"Mom, You're Incredible! is an incredible book. I can't think of a more uplifting message for new or veteran moms. It's packed with real-world encouragement from a mom who has faced the trials and triumphs of mothering and seen God's hand throughout. I guarantee that if you read this book, it will bless your life."

> John Trent, Ph.D.
> Author/Speaker
> President of Encouraging Words

"This book's overall message is a wake-up call! Reading it, I was reminded of my priority and value as a mother. I just loved the enthusiasm the author shares within these pages about incredible moms!"

> Jan Dravecky
> Co-author, with husband Dave,
> of *When You Can't Come Back*

"Any woman who can give a child its life deserves our respect. But the woman who is willing to commit the time, tears, and toil to give that child's life meaning deserves a standing ovation. *Mom, You're Incredible!* is a long-overdue 'standing O' for the groomers of the future and the true stewards of eternity."

> Tim Kimmel
> Author of *Powerful Personalities*
> and *Little House on the Freeway*

"No test tube or radar screen can adequately describe what is probably the world's toughest job, but Linda Weber threads through the maze of 21st-century unease with a can-do kind of confidence. Her book makes mothering believable for the fearful first-timer and boosts the stressed-out veteran back into orbit."

> Howard and Jeanne Hendricks
> Christian Leadership Center
> Dallas Theological Seminary

"If you have never really had good, solid, emotionally rich mothering, how do you know how to move into your own children's lives in deep, effective ways? *Mom, You're Incredible!* gives down-to-earth, well-balanced guidance to encourage you in fulfilling your eternally important role."

Pamela Reeve
Women's Ministries Advisor
Multnomah Bible College
and Seminary
Author of *Faith Is . . .*

"What mom hasn't felt the deflating voices of discouragement? Take heart, *Mom, You're Incredible!* is guaranteed to lift your spirits, boost your value, and exalt your role as 'mother.' Linda Weber will challenge you to take a fresh approach to being an effective mom. Put this book by your nightstand—it will give you courage!"

Dennis and Barbara Rainey
FamilyLife Ministry

"Motherhood is in trouble today, and moms everywhere need all the encouragement they can get. Along comes Linda Weber's inspiring book *Mom, You're Incredible!* to make readers laugh and cry. A must read!"

Brenda Hunter, Ph.D.
Psychologist and author
of *What Every Mother Needs to
Know* and *Home By Choice*

"*Mom, You're Incredible!* is a heart-to-heart love letter, a gift of encouragement, perspective, perseverance, and joy for every mother. You will enjoy Linda Weber's warm, personal, practical, insightful look at the supernatural motherhood journey! And your children will thank you."

Susan Smith
Psychologist

Mom
You're Incredible!

To Karin,

Enjoy being a mom to your new baby boy!

my love,
Linda Staten

Mom
You're Incredible!

Linda Weber

PUBLISHING
Colorado Springs, Colorado

MOM, YOU'RE INCREDIBLE

Library of Congress Cataloging-in-Publication Data
Weber, Linda, 1947-
    Mom, you're incredible / Linda Weber.
       p.   cm.
    ISBN 1-56179-221-7
    1. Mothers. 2. Mother and child.
HQ759.W383 1994
306.874'3—dc20   93-39465
                                               CIP

Published by Focus on the Family Publishing, Colorado Springs, Colorado 80995.

Distributed in the U.S.A. and Canada by Word Books, Dallas, Texas.

Unless otherwise noted, Scripture quotations are from the Holy Bible, New International Version, copyright © 1973, 1978, 1984 by the International Bible Society.

Editor: Larry Weeden
Cover Design: Jeff Stoddard

Printed in the United States of America

94 95 96 97 98 99 / 10 9 8 7 6 5 4 3 2 1

Dedication

I dedicate this book to you:

the mothers out there who deserve much affirmation for the
influence you bear and the history you shape.

my tender warrior husband, Stu, who gave me the privilege of
sharing parenthood and is himself a precious gift to me.

my three wonderful sons, Kent, Blake, and Ryan, valued treasures
of my heart who gave me the name for this book.

my mother, June, a gift from God who gave me, even more than
biological life, a nurtured spirit.

my future daughters-in-law,

and to Jami Lyn, the gem already found and to whom I give my
apron strings . . .

Apron Strings

These apron strings I give you
from winding 'round my heart;
entwined around my little boy,
and now they're cut apart.

I give them to you, Jami Lyn,
Blake's yours to have and hold;
I promise there are no strings attached
so your love, indeed, unfolds.

That place of being number 1
      I pass to you, sweet girl;
although he's special to this mom,
      his wife now makes life swirl.

You know you've got a winner
      in this champion Blaker;
we feel he's chosen of like kind
      to please our great Maker.

We've prayed for you this man to take
      your vows till death do us part;
commitment to each other speaks
      of how you are so smart.

Now when I cut these strings away
      to replace this cord of love,
I wrapped my heart around you both
      'til God calls me from above.

We can't o'erlook the future,
      Weber generations yet to come,
those little children announcing gladly,
      "Mommy, Mommy, you're awesome."

Jami Lyn, we do accept you
      into our big family;
may we seek the God of heaven
      to live each day eternally!

I love you, Jami Lyn.
Mom Weber

(Written by Linda Weber and presented to her new daughter-in-law at Blake and Jami Lyn's wedding rehearsal dinner, August 13, 1993.)

Contents

Acknowledgments

————— ✦ —————

Dennis Rainey, national director of FamilyLife, inspired this book when he encouraged those of us on the speaking team to pursue publishing in the areas of our strengths. Although I had started developing other ideas, my husband, Stu, said, "Mothering needs to be first." Thank you, Dennis and Stu, for getting the ball rolling.

Kent, Blake, and Ryan, our three sons, have been most encouraging in this process. They have believed in me. They have recognized that a significant measure of the personal security they each enjoy is derived from the mothering they received in childhood. Their words have kept me on course: "Mom, you're incredible! Now write that book." Thank you, guys!

My own mom, June Lininger, has always been my cheerleader. Mom, you've encouraged me to "go for it" in whatever area I wished to pursue. Thanks for your confidence, for following this project with such prayerful enthusiasm, and for spurring me on to the very end.

Al Janssen, Focus on the Family knew what it was doing when it hired you as director of book publishing. Thank you for sticking with me. You heard my story and encouraged a proposal. And in spite of having to return it to me more than once, you continued to tell me what to do next, and you coached me all the way to the successful completion of this mission.

Joan Petersen, your endless hours of cheerfully typing revision after revision, even at the oddest times, are forever etched in my heart. I could not have done this without you, good friend. How can I ever adequately thank you?

Steve Tucker, your skillful rewriting and extensive work with me over the manuscript was a major factor in seeing this published. Thank you, Steve, for wanting to see it happen. You're great!

Larry Weeden, my editor, you are a gem. From your first hearing of this book's message, you were a supporter. Thank you for your role in selecting this book for publication, for your sweet spirit, for your always-positive attitude, and for your polished editing skills. An author could not ask for a better editor and partner.

And there are others to thank. So many gave me informative interviews. So many have read and evaluated the material for me. And I will never forget my prayer warrior friends who watched over it all. Thanks to all of you for the intense interest, time, and care you gave me.

And to my special partners, Linda Campbell and Cheryl McCamman, I owe so much. Your extensive work and love for this project have meant the world to me. You're both amazing—and incredible moms! Thanks, too, Linda, for insisting we celebrate even before we knew this book was a publishing reality.

For the many others who have been a part of the development of this book, my thanks to you all.

Finally, I'm especially grateful to our almighty God for allowing me the privilege of being part of this large team in taking the message of the value of motherhood to a society so desperately in need of it. May He be honored above all.

Preface

How is it that motherhood, the nurturing and building up of children, has taken such a nosedive in honor and respect in the last 20 years?

Whether it's the wounded soldier on the battlefield calling "Mother" or the young player on the sideline mouthing "Hi, Mom" to the TV camera, in moments of distress or elation, where do people's minds always turn? To Mom. No one can take her place. No tie in life is as strong or lasting as that of a child to his mother.

Why, then, don't we see much good press for motherhood these days? Television doesn't seem to know how to portray moms. Teachers often encourage young girls not to "waste" their lives just being moms. And women are continually encouraged to assert their intelligence and influence everywhere but in the home. Sadly, no one seems to see the connection: Minimize the importance of motherhood, and witness the decline of the family and society.

Someone needs to stand up and say, "Come on, let's use our heads. Moms are essential to everything from their children's self-image to the societal standards those children will one day shape. The success and well-being of our children are almost totally dependent on our success as moms. Being a mom is the most strategic, pivotal role in any society."

How could such an essential and noble commitment have been so depreciated, discredited, and discounted? What a calling! What a responsibility! What an honor!

This book is a tribute to moms everywhere, for they deserve great recognition for shaping history. Mom, you are to be elevated for the incredible importance you have in the positive development of future generations. I esteem you for the perseverance you display in fulfilling daily the thousands of tasks necessary to ensure that you leave a healthy heritage.

It is essential that you learn to feel good about who you are and what you do. You're not expendable. You're not missing out on life. You're the very bedrock of life. You should feel terrific about that.

As you read the following pages, may you catch your value in a new and powerful way. May you tingle with excitement as you strive to influence the world through your children. And may your newly realized worth help whisk away any lingering clouds of doubt that even consider entrance into your life.

My purpose here is for you to come to believe anew that you're invaluable, and to raise your effectiveness to an all-time high. Mom, you're incredible!

1

Do Well-Adjusted Kids Just Happen?

*lot is expected of moms today. I want to say things* were better for my mother. I suppose they were in a way. Being a mom was considered a full-time effort back then. No one chided, "You don't belong at home. Get out in the world and make a difference." She was never challenged to opt for a different focus or to build a career. In her generation, if you were a mom, that's just who you were, first and foremost. Anything else was extra— and secondary.

On the other hand, things were a lot harder for Mom. She had three children to raise and an angry, abusive husband to contend with until he finally abandoned us. The responsibility of providing for the family always fell on her shoulders. If we were going to eat, she had to work. And back then, the job market for women was limited, both in choices and in pay. As I recall, she never made more than $200 a month.

We lived in an apple orchard in a small structure built to house migrant workers. A couch sat against one wall of our tiny living room, and an old upright piano covered the opposite wall. If I stood in the center of the room, I could reach out and touch both pieces at the same time.

Cold floors. No carpet. An oil stove for heat. The rent was $25 a month. We used spare apple boxes for cupboards and dressers and covered them with old tea towels. We were allowed to collect the fallen apples and added to them the wild asparagus that grew here and there among the trees.

When the school year began, if we kids were lucky, we'd get to choose one pair of shoes to last us the year. Naturally, our wardrobe selection left more than a little to be desired. Most of our clothes were hand-me-downs from other families. Occasionally, our grandmother would buy Easter dresses for my sister and me. When I got into high school, a friend's mother made clothes for me so I could look like everyone else.

What Mom lacked in wealth, however, she made up for in character. She was a devout woman with a steady, thankful heart. She loved her God and read the Bible morning and night. She lived what she learned and never did anything she feared was wrong—not even reusing a postage stamp that had been missed by the cancellation stamp. She trusted that God could handle anything we had to face, and she told us time and again, "God knows our need. He loves us. He'll provide."

For all her sacrifices, for all she did without, Mom never made us feel it was our fault or that she was missing out on something. She never gave the impression she was "stuck" rais-ing the three of us. She never gave those impressions because she never felt that way. She understood what more women today need to comprehend.

Mom was giving her all to one thing—mothering. Working was a necessary part of that, but her priorities were never con-fused. She couldn't provide all the things we thought we needed. She couldn't sit back and enjoy much leisure. But she could do one thing as well as anyone, regardless of resources or status: She could be a full-time, all-out mom. She could invest her life in her children. And that she did with passion.

We got by. Mom kept a positive attitude while she focused on the *heart* and *spirit*. That's what she developed in us, and that's the need for today.

Because she had a focus, because she knew one thing was more important than anything else, she has three successful,

Well-adjusted kids
come from families in
which mothering is
seen as a complex,
beautiful challenge
worthy of everything
Mom can give to it.

well-adjusted children who adore her. Her son is a pastor. Her two daughters married pastors. And all of us are now raising children with the same passion and focus Mom showed when we were young.

A lot *is* expected of moms today. But well-adjusted kids don't just happen. Moms, we need to see mothering—developing the hearts and spirits—as the main thing, the central focus of our efforts. And as the German proverb says, "The main thing is that the main thing always remains the main thing."

Well-adjusted kids come from families in which mothering is seen as a complex, beautiful challenge worthy of everything Mom can give to it. Mothering shapes lives and attitudes, one way or the other.

That's not to say you have to stay home all the time to be a decent mother. Mom worked at outside jobs. She had to. Today, more moms than ever have to fit work into their schedules. But Mom understood the importance of giving her *best* efforts to what was most important—her children.

Despite all the demands on a working mom in the 1960s, she understood the need to be there during the rehearsals of life—the learning stages of our youth—so that when the curtain went up for each of us, we could perform well. That meant setting the stage by developing character and confidence. Though Mom didn't give us a high standard of living, she gave us a high standard of life. It didn't matter how many rooms our little migrant house had. What mattered was what went on in those rooms.

Over the years, it seems some of our common sense for mothering has been lost. Maybe it's because so many young mothers no longer enjoy the proximity of extended family, where skills and insights are passed from older moms to younger ones. Maybe it's because we think, before we have kids, that knowing how to be a good mother and having the right answers just come naturally. But we soon learn better.

The truth is, motherhood can't be discounted. It can't be devalued. And it can't be approached casually. We're willing to take lessons and expend energy for everything from aerobics to budgeting to computers. If we want to do well at mothering, we're going to have to study it as well.

Motherhood develops the heart and the spirit of our kids; it nurtures self-esteem and emotional security. Kids who have great mothers enjoy self-confidence and a sense of direction for their lives.

Doesn't it just make sense to give mothering your best efforts? Well-adjusted kids take an investment of your life in theirs—the best of your life, not the leftovers.

Mom, if you don't do it, who will? If this isn't all-important, next to the nurturing of your marriage, what is? The challenge is yours. Will your family enjoy the positive results of your efforts?

If you haven't done it before, won't you commit yourself right now to making the main thing the main thing? What better legacy could you leave to your children than your full investment in their growing-up years?

If you've already made that commitment, take pride in your decision. Affirm it. Motherhood is the greatest cause you could follow, and you've given yourself to it. Now do all you can to live out that decision with excellence!

2

Is There Light at the End of This Tunnel?

*inally*, *a night out of the house. No laundry. No demands. Just some relaxation, some time for me.*

Then came the emergency phone call.

"Mom, you gotta come home. Ryan climbed into the grandfather clock, and it fell over, and the clock's all over the floor, and Ryan's crying."

That kid! My clock! My night out! Good grief, Lord!

Ryan was always into everything. Can't you just imagine this little kid exploring the house, looking for a place to hide? Then he found it. The clock. The antique grandfather clock. The *beautiful* clock we'd brought back from Germany after a tour in the army. *My* clock. My pride and joy. One of the few things of grace and beauty in a struggling young family's home furnished mostly in early in-law.

Now, as Ryan had boosted himself into the cabinet to hide behind the pendulum, the whole thing had come crashing down.

Would there ever be any light at the end of this tunnel?

That wasn't the first time the question had crossed my mind. In fact, there were lots of those times when the boys were little. Their dad was in seminary. Money was tight, and luxuries were nonexistent. We were new in town and didn't know anyone in our neighborhood. There was absolutely no money for baby-sitters, and I rarely got any help with the kids from my husband, Stu, who was overwhelmed with classes, studying, and holding down two jobs. Talk about the housebound mother! We barely had enough for the essentials, and even our gas money had to be rationed. I took care of the boys, cooked, washed, and did the unending housework.

Erma Bombeck compares housework to stringing beads with no knot at the end. That's how I felt, and with no room in our budget for diversions, I felt as if my whole life were just stringing beads.

It was "just me and the boys"—and it was bleak. I tried to take a class of my own. I *needed* an outlet. But it didn't work. Things just wouldn't stretch. At first, I tried to make it happen. Then I saw the effect all that stress could have on our boys, and I let it go.

I can look back now, see it all in perspective, and laugh about it, but there were times when I felt motherhood was sapping everything from me. My time wasn't my own, my body wasn't my own, demands were placed on every waking hour—often even my sleep was sacrificed. Something as simple as a leisurely, uninterrupted bath seemed to be an unrealistic expectation. "Oh, please," I'd sigh, "don't I get any breaks?"

One cold morning, as we headed for church, one of the babies burped up his breakfast all over my coat. The stain and aroma permeated it. I didn't have a second coat, so I went to church without one.

I took the coat to the cleaners the next day. When I went to pick it up a couple of days later, it was ruined. The dry cleaner refused to accept any responsibility or pay for the damages. He said it was a manufacturing defect and suggested I return it to the store where I bought it. But we were in Oregon, and I had purchased the coat when we were in Germany. Now it seemed I couldn't even have a warm coat of my own for winter. How discouraging!

Reluctantly, I thought of the $35 given to me for my birthday. I'd been saving it for something special. I wanted to spend part of it for a new Bible that would cost $15. But where would I be able to buy a winter dress coat for the remaining $20? Even if I used the entire $35, it would be a miracle to find a good coat for that price.

I had to have one, however, so I took all the money and went shopping at a large store that specialized in coats, hoping I could find a bargain. Amazingly, the man who attended to me was the owner. When he learned of my dilemma, he graciously offered me a very nice (and expensive) coat and charged me just $19.99.

Things didn't turn out so badly after all. I got a nice coat, I was able to buy the new Bible I had been wanting, and I learned that things often aren't as hopeless as they might seem.

That story means a lot to me. But if I were in the same situation today, some people would tell me, "Well, it's obvious you just need to go to work. Your whole family will be better off if you have more income. And you need to do it for you, too. You don't have to settle for being a maid and a bottle washer. Everyone needs fulfillment. Get a job. The boys will be fine. Kids are resilient. In fact, it'll be good for them."

That can sound pretty convincing when you're being pressured or at a low point.

A friend of mine was an excellent teacher—one of the best around. I remember when she had her first baby. She was so excited, so enthusiastic about staying home with her child. But her principal at school and her fellow teachers just wouldn't give up. She *couldn't* waste all that talent and just stay home. She *needed* to go back to work. It was the "right" thing to do.

In times like that, you need to be able to look down the road beyond today's obstacles and see your goal. (My friend did and resisted the pressure to return to work.) You need perspective to make those critical choices. You need to remind yourself, *This is important. It's not a waste of my life or talents. The future of these kids depends on me.*

That's what I did, and it made a difference. My boys have written me numerous notes of thanks over the years for majoring on mothering instead of being distracted by other pursuits. They noticed. It had an impact that they continue to appreciate.

If we're not willing to empty ourselves to fill up our children, who will be?

I received a desperate phone call one day recently. My friend Susan was in over her head with a toddler and an infant. Susan's a capable, intelligent woman—a trained psychologist. But she wasn't feeling very capable then. In fact, she was ready to throw in the towel. This mothering business was for the birds, she said. It had been a long way from the halls of academia to the changing table, and at the moment it seemed like the wrong direction.

She pleaded incompetence. She begged for escape. She felt trapped, breathless. The endless clutter was closing in on her, and she was ready to run.

"I'm tired *all* the time," she said. "I can't get on top of anything. These kids have insatiable needs and demands. And even they don't know why they're crying."

Sound familiar?

By her own admission, Susan was "freaking out." (Psychologists can be so clinical.) The two-year-old seemed bent on destroying everything in his path, the baby never stopped screaming ... and then there was that bottomless diaper pail.

"Help!" she begged.

That week, I'd received letters from our two older boys, who were away in college. I read the letters to her. They told how thankful the boys were for me, how much they were coming to realize and appreciate all my sacrifices, my taxi service, and my time spent with them. As my oldest, Kent, wrote, "I'm convinced that the main reason I've grown up, developed, and matured with so few problems and so many advantages is that you always loved me and looked out for me the way you did."

By the time I finished reading, Susan was crying—not because she couldn't take it anymore, but because some of her perspective had been restored. She had seen beyond the day's obstacles to her goals for tomorrow.

Now that my boys are pretty much independent, I sometimes work part-time in a department store. When we have a special sale and I see the women stampeding into the aisles as the doors first open, I'm reminded of how I often felt stampeded by the demands of mothering little ones.

Susan was caught up in that, too—riding herd on the "wild years" when the investment is just being made, long before you begin to enjoy any of the dividends. In those times, you need reminders of "the main thing." You need a vision to focus upon. You need to know, even though it may not look as if your efforts are bearing fruit, that they will pay off one day, and that the chances are excellent that they will provide great satisfaction. Everything you do has its impact.

For instance, all three of our boys love sports—all sports. About the time they reached junior high age, I took each of them to the local courts to teach them the game of tennis. I spent hour after hour hitting the ball, returning volleys, and helping them develop a serve. We'd keep at it until we were both exhausted. I don't know which was harder, hitting all the balls or dishing out all the encouragement.

Blake, in particular, had a hard time. He'd begin missing the ball, making mistakes, and then he'd get down on himself. His racket would drop, his head would go down, and his shoulders would droop.

"Come on," I'd say, "try it again. You'll get it." Day after day, I was his cheerleader. What a struggle! I thought I'd collapse. *Could this possibly ever be worth all the hassle?* I sometimes wondered.

Then Blake's game began to click. He improved steadily. As he and Kent went into high school, they played on the school team together and became district champions as doubles partners. After Kent graduated, Blake found another partner, and they repeated the championship. Now both the boys have gone on to play competitively in college. Kent was nationally ranked and was named an All-American and a national scholar/athlete. Ryan, the youngest, was a varsity letterman on his high school team for four years besides being named most valuable player time and again.

Was the effort worth it? The boys think so. The tennis scholarships say so. Their college teams have traveled extensively throughout the United States and visited several foreign countries, experiences we could never have provided. Kent has even worked as a tennis pro, earning money for graduate school.

Most of all, the boys have developed character. Hard work, perseverance, acquired skills, self-discipline, learning to win and lose gracefully—what good lessons! What positive results! They feel good about themselves. They have the satisfaction and pleasure of their accomplishments, and they have confidence in life. And it all started by taking the time to hit the ball, build them up, hit the ball again, and build them up again.

How different might their lives have been if I had given in to the stampede of demands and decided other things were more important?

Mom, don't underestimate your impact. Abe Lincoln once said he considered his mother to be the person chiefly responsible for

You need to know,
even though it may
not look as if your
efforts are bearing
fruit, that they will
pay off one day.
Everything you do
has its impact.

all he was or ever hoped to become.[1] She was just a poor, simple, country mother. But she taught him about sacrifice. She taught him to read. And she gave him a healthy self-image that sustained him through a lifetime of challenges, disappointments, and defeats. That's quite a legacy, especially when you learn she died when Lincoln was just ten years old.

Thomas Edison's mother taught him at home after she learned his teachers considered him to have inferior ability. "My mother was the making of me," he said later in life. "She was so true, so sure of me; and I felt that I had someone to live for, someone I must not disappoint."[2]

You don't have to be someone of note to make a noteworthy impact on someone else's life. Just be faithful in your efforts, keep focused on the main thing, and watch what happens. History is written by little people in little places doing what they should.

Is there light at the end of the tunnel? You bet there is! Keep believing. Keep focusing. Come on, hit the ball, and build them up.

3

Did You Say *Just* a Mother?

*onna's husband called from work to tell her they* had been invited to a dinner party—a command performance. The founder and the CEO of his company often held these affairs to encourage the work force. And when they asked, you came.

Dinner out sounded pretty good: fancy tables, beautiful flowers, pleasant music, and pampering service from handsome waiters in black tuxedos. But a company dinner party . . . that was different. The founder was a millionaire, the CEO a well-known socialite. That meant dinner would be very elegant and very intimidating.

With three preschoolers underfoot, Donna didn't have much time to worry about hairstyles and the latest fashions. At their present income level, it wouldn't have mattered much anyway. But this was a command performance, and feeling out of place wasn't an acceptable excuse for declining. So off they went.

The restaurant lived up to all expectations. A harpist sat at the end of the table and played throughout the evening. The guests were surrounded by waiters attentive to every whim and desire. It was all very elegant, indeed.

Donna had come to the party feeling ill at ease. Then, as everyone was introduced and seated, she found herself placed next to the CEO. He turned, smiled, and asked her, "What do you do?"

She quietly explained that she was a mother of three preschoolers.

"Oh," he said in response. Donna's sure that's what he said, because that was the last word he spoke to her the entire evening. He wasn't sarcastic or purposely rude. It's just that he obviously thought she had nothing of interest to contribute to the evening's discussion, so he turned to the person on his other side, and that's where he directed his attention the rest of the evening.

Can you imagine how Donna felt? Out of style, out of place, and now out of the conversation. Can't you just feel her self-esteem melting away? After all, she was just a mother.

Just a mother?

It's really a shame the English language isn't more expressive. I wish *mother* wasn't such an all-inclusive word. There should be one term for *child-bearer* and a totally different word for *child-raiser and nurturer*. These days, it seems there are plenty of the former but fewer and fewer of the latter.

Sometimes it seems to me that respect for mothering is almost on its way to extinction, with hardly anyone noticing. If some animal out in the wilderness were as endangered, it would be on the national news. Years ago, it was a small, fresh-water fish called the snail darter in Tennessee. Now it's the spotted owl in the Pacific Northwest.

Mom, don't let society's lack of respect for your work get you down. Don't let anyone convince you it's not worth doing, no matter what the cost. And please remember, the issue isn't really whether you have a job outside the home. My mother did, and after my boys reached a certain age, I did, too. The problem is that people think you *need* a job to be a whole person, to use your brain, or to carry your weight.

Donna should have told Mr. Big she was director of health, education, and welfare. She should have said she was secretary of the treasury and the head of public affairs. She should have told him she was chairman of the house rules committee. She should have responded, "Jerry, I'm responsible to teach my kids everything from how to chew food to how to drive a car. What do *you* do all day?"

To put it another way, the issue is not whether there's an outside job in your schedule, but what's most important in your schedule. If you're honest with yourself, look at your schedule, and conclude that mothering really has become secondary, you're going to have to expect secondary results.

If you choose to work outside the home, make sure you have your priorities well in focus. And do so understanding just how much you're committing yourself to. Most people don't realize all a mother is called upon to do. A fan of Ann Landers wrote:

> I'm so tired of all those ignorant people who come up to my husband and ask him if his wife has a full-time job or if she's "just a housewife." Please print this letter and shed some light on this sorely under-valued occupation. Thank you. Here is my job description.
>
> I'm a wife, mother, friend, confidante, personal advisor, lover, referee, peacemaker, housekeeper, laundress, chauffeur, interior decorator, gardener, painter, wallpaperer, dog groomer, veterinarian, manicurist, barber, seamstress, appointment manager, financial planner, bookkeeper, money manager, personal secretary, teacher, disciplinarian, entertainer, psychoanalyst, nurse, diagnostician, public relations expert, dietitian and nutritionist, baker, chef, fashion coordinator and letter writer for both sides of the family.
>
> I am also a travel agent, speech therapist, plumber and automobile maintenance and repair expert. During the course of the day, I am supposed to be cheerful, look radiant and jump in the sack on a moment's notice.
>
> From the studies done, it would cost more than $75,000 a year to replace me. I took time out of my busy day to write this letter, Ann, because there are

still ignorant people who believe a housewife is nothing more than a babysitter who sits on her behind all day and looks at soap operas.

If I could afford to pay someone to do all the things that I do, I would be delighted to go back to working an eight-hour day with an hour for lunch and two fifteen-minute breaks.

What do I get out of my job in the absence of a salary? Joy, happiness, hugs, kisses, smiles, love, self-respect and pride in knowing that I have done a full day's work to ensure the physical and emotional well-being of those I love.

Now if you still want to classify me as just a housewife, go ahead.[1]

You can sure identify with her, can't you? I just love to read her letter to women when I speak on mothering. Invariably, that mom's message brings great applause. Everyone identifies. Everyone understands. It rings so true.

Sometimes, when I think about all I'm supposed to do to launch my kids safely into this world, I feel as if I'm trying to launch the space shuttle Discovery. The atmosphere my kids are destined for seems no less dangerous, and the thousands of details that need attention seem as important as any NASA research, training, or construction project. Too much is at stake to get sloppy or neglect my responsibilities.

Moms, remember, every mother is a working mother. Can we devote too much time to mothering? Can we be too prepared, know too much? Can we possibly be overqualified? As an essential partner in marriage or in any business, the more expertise we bring, the more time and diligence we dedicate to the task at hand, the better return we receive.

But what if your time and energy are already maxed out by demands outside your home? How will your child's inner needs be met—even be recognized? The more needs that go unmet,

I've used all my
abilities to undergird
my family. Some
day, in some way,
you'll have to use
all of yours.

the more problems will arise. If a mother's life gets too crowded with demands, some things will be left undone. Isn't it better to do some careful evaluating now and make the choices of what gets the attention and what is put aside? Without making conscious choices, things happen by default, and the urgent things may get more attention than the important.

Every family is different. Every set of circumstances is unique. Just how you go about dividing responsibilities with your husband or chores among your children is up to you. The point is for you to ensure that your family is cared for in a healthy, balanced manner.

Will we mothers be fully appreciated for all our efforts? For now, probably not. Unfortunately, just when moms with young families are sacrificing the most, dads are going through their toughest years of establishing a career, making a place for themselves, and earning a decent living. They may not have the energy left to notice all we do. But take heart, because husbands get smarter as they get older, as we all do.

If you need instant gratification for your mothering, you might become disappointed. But over the years, you'll receive more appreciation than you can imagine. Don't focus on not being appreciated today. Self-sacrifice has always been a trait of great mothers. For now, *you* may just have to remind *yourself* of the importance of your role and the importance of the ones you love who are at stake. Someday, your family will show its appreciation.

Don't feel as if you have to check your brains at the door, either. I've used all my abilities to undergird my family. Some day, in some way, you'll have to use all of yours.

My sister, Judy, and her husband, Rick, took their clan out for breakfast one Saturday morning at a camp where Rick worked. Kyle was five, Bryan was three, Eric was two, and within a couple of months, a fourth child was due. After breakfast, Judy and the kids returned home to get ready for a party, and Rick left to do some work.

While Judy wrapped a package, the boys asked to go outside to play. She would only be busy for a couple of minutes, so out they went.

For some reason, the boys wandered farther from the house than ever by themselves—all the way to a nearby pond. One at a time, they each tried to jump over a little dam holding back runoff from a recent rainstorm. Kyle made it. Bryan made it. But Eric, the littlest, didn't and fell into deep water. Big brother Kyle jumped in to save him. Kyle made it to Eric's still body, tried to pull on him, and yelled to Bryan, "He's too heavy! Go get Mom!" Soon they both disappeared under the muddy water.

By this time, Judy had finished wrapping the present and called to the boys. When they didn't respond, she went looking for them. She hurried toward the pond, where she remembered their trikes had been left the day before. There she found Bryan in shock, unable to tell her much about what had happened except that the other two were "dying in the water." Judy, dressed and seven months pregnant, scoured the edges of the pond and then jumped into the water, searching frantically along the muddy bottom for the boys. She became stuck, pulled herself free with weeds that edged the pond, looked into heaven, and prayed loudly, "Please don't take both!"

Just as she was looking down, Eric surfaced out in the middle of the pond. She swam out to him, pulled him from the water, and began CPR. Fortunately, Judy was skilled in the life-saving procedure, and she was able to revive him. But his big brother and rescuer, Kyle, was lodged below and drowned. What a horrible experience! What a terrible memory!

Judy's instincts as a mom took over that day. She entered that murky pond to save her boys. Nothing else mattered—not her clothes, not her condition, not the danger of uncertain, murky water. She had only one thought on her mind—rescuing her sons.

It's sad that her valiant efforts that day were overshadowed by their terrible loss, our family's terrible loss. But she did everything possible, and she had made a great difference. She had saved a life.[2]

That may seem like an extreme example, but stories help us remember important points, and I want to leave you with this thought: I hope you'll never be called upon to save your child's life like Judy, but you *are* called upon to shape it. And you know what? In the long run, shaping your child's life *is* saving it.

Did you say you were "just a mother"? Oh no, my dear, you're not. You're so very much more! (For a more extensive look at all the things that demand your attention, please refer to the appendix, "What in the World Do I Do All Day?")

4

Can We
Really Make
a Difference?

*he newspaper article said she was a beautiful girl, a* high-school student, and an exceptional basketball player. She came from a good home, and life was promising. We'll call her Jenny.

Jenny lived for basketball—until her injury. Being sidelined for part of the season seemed almost unbearable. Learning she would never play again was crushing. The family was devastated.

To somehow make up for her loss, her parents, who had both been poor when they were growing up, decided to give Jenny what they had lacked—things. And because of their acquired wealth, they gave her many extravagant things.

Clothes overflowed her closet. Cars filled the driveway. A private airplane took them wherever they wanted. They even bought a hot air balloon. Jenny lacked nothing, her parents thought. Surely this would dispel her disappointment.

But instead of rising above the situation, Jenny fell into depression. She felt unimportant. Her self-esteem collapsed. Her temper tantrums became unmanageable.

One Sunday morning, Jenny's mother went to Jenny's bedroom to wake her for breakfast. The girl lay face down. She was wearing her prom dress, her bare feet hanging over the end of the bed. Her mom reached down to massage a foot to wake her and found her skin was cold. Jenny had taken her life.

"We did everything for the girl," her parents said later in stunned disbelief. How could it have happened? She was young and pretty. She had wealth and a promising life ahead. What more could anyone have done?

How can we know if we're making a difference in our children's lives? What *will* make a real difference?

In a coloring book, it doesn't matter how simple or complex the drawings are; they always seem flat, lifeless, and two-dimensional. But when color is added to the page, it brings life and dimension. Until the color is added, the outlined characters merely exhibit potential. Color brings completion.

Kids are a lot like those outlined drawings. The house they live in, the things they own—the bikes, balls, toys, or clothes—the schools they've attended, and the training they've received are only black boundary lines on a white background. If that's all there is, the figures remain flat, lifeless, two-dimensional. What may be missing are the colors of self-esteem, spiritual and emotional security, self-image, and confidence.

Jenny had all the bold lines, but evidently the colors inside were too pale to sustain her. She hadn't grieved her loss to the point of healing. Her heart and soul had become sick. She lost hope in the midst of an abundance of things. Obviously, her parents had tried to help her overcome her disappointment, but from a distance, it appears as if more time was spent drawing new lines rather than bringing color to what was already there.

By majoring on mothering, we can add the color to our kids' lives.

Dads understand lines, boundaries, and borders. They focus on goals like providing for their kids' skates, braces, or college tuition. Dads will give their lives for lines.

Moms, on the other hand, understand nuance, nurturing, and developing. Moms color in the blank spaces. With our more sensitive natures, we're more attuned to what hurts, what's wrong, what intimidates. With that understanding, provided we focus our attention on mothering and spend our best efforts on our kids, we can provide the color and shading that bring depth and dimension to their lives.

What we build into our
kids' hearts underpins
what they live out in
their lives. It has little
to do with how much
we give them.
It has everything to do
with how we make
them *feel*.

Maybe it was good that our family didn't have much in our early years. Because we were on such a shoestring budget, I couldn't get distracted pursuing too many physical concerns—the things I could buy next for the kids. Instead, my focus was on creating a comfortable, encouraging environment to grow in. I saw how unique each boy was. I saw his individual needs. The more I worked at understanding how each one ticked so I could help them all grow, the more success we enjoyed.

Blake received a letter from a friend recently saying the thing that stood out most about him was that he obviously cared a lot more about people than things. How rewarding to me! Blake was reproducing what had been planted at home. The coloring showed. Someone could see his depth.

What we build into our kids' hearts underpins what they live out in their lives. It has little to do with how much we give them. It has everything to do with how we make them *feel*.

Kent, working as a tennis pro, has seen the needs of those who live in wealth and luxury yet feel unloved, uncared for, unfulfilled. Elaborate bold lines. But no color.

My high-school Latin teacher always challenged us to "name six" whenever we tried to answer one of her questions. She wanted six examples or reasons for every answer we gave. It was her way of making sure we understood all aspects of what we were talking about. Perhaps it would be good to "name six" for you in answering why our best efforts are needed and really can make a difference. There will be some overlap between the six, but I hope that by looking at these issues from various perspectives, you'll gain a fresh appreciation for the impact you can have.

1. Kids need to feel worthwhile and accepted.

We communicate acceptance to our children as we let them be who they are—as we, for example, let a four-year-old act like a four-year-old. Not expecting perfection or even advanced behavior says, "I accept you now, not only after you change or grow up." And such acceptance without conditions is essential to a healthy self-esteem.

Mom, even when there are grass stains, a broken window, spilled syrup, or stupid behavior, our proper attitude toward the inner person of our children nourishes the good feelings they need about being accepted.

When we focus on our kids in a positive way, helping them develop self-esteem and confidence, every aspect of their lives is affected. Being around for our kids during the day, being available, dispels loneliness. Smiles and hugs are comforting. Signs of approval encourage and strengthen. They create comfort zones. And being included in our activities makes our kids feel they're really worthwhile. It's all pretty simple and obvious.

Dr. Ray Guarendi has written lessons he learned from observing 100 of America's happiest families. He says,

> Making ourselves accessible to our children forges more than a durable family bond. It also provides them with a sense of security. No matter what life away from home deals them, no matter what risks they take and lose, no matter what outside supports they watch crumble beneath them, the unquestionable presence of their parents remains. The certainty that there is always a place to gather and regroup will bolster a youngster's self-confidence as he prepares for another run at the world. . . . Nothing can more quietly and surely build a child's self-confidence than knowing his parents will be present and supportive, whenever, however.[1]

Guarendi goes on to say, "Attentive presence is a quiet way to say, 'I love you. You are most special in my life.' " He tells how easy it is to affirm a child's worth. We can simply look up from what we're doing and listen to a choppy version of a joke we heard years ago, showing interest and demonstrating our acceptance.[2]

In *Parents* magazine, Ellie Kahan quotes Dr. Barbara Berger, a child and adolescent therapist in New York, who says, "Self-esteem is a child's pride in himself. To have high self-esteem, a child must feel both lovable and capable. He must believe that he is worthwhile, has something to offer, and can handle himself and his environment."[3]

Writer Kahan goes on to say, "The degree to which a child feels lovable and capable affects every area of his life and future. It's an important factor in determining a child's ability to be creative, relate to others, and to achieve."[4]

When your children feel accepted and see you readily accept others, they'll accept others more easily. They'll feel confident to reach out and draw them in. Since our boys grew up in a pastor's home, they were exposed to many guests, from missionaries and nationally-known speakers to battered mothers and other people in crisis. It's been fun to see how Blake has been influenced by our acceptance of him and others.

Blake has never met a stranger and has rarely been intimidated. He has invited his college president and visiting international speakers to his roommate's house for burgers. He's looked up the addresses of famous athletes and stopped by just to meet them and learn from them. He's definitely enjoying life from the basis of feeling good about himself and accepted by others.

We've also noticed that making each of our sons feel accepted has minimized the natural temptation to compare themselves to one another or to doubt themselves. They're different sizes, with different interests and skills. But because they've felt accepted for who they are, they haven't felt the need to match up to or better one another.

Believe it or not, I've also found that how you accept your children will be reflected in how your children accept you. A friend's daughter works with high-school girls. Again and again, she sees girls pulling away from their parents when they leave the house. She told her mom, "I know why I didn't have that problem. You accepted me." And as a result, she can accept her mom as well.

In contrast, we can learn from a common thread in the lives of hardened criminals. The famous ones and the ones we read about almost daily in our newspapers reveal that they *weren't* accepted by their parents and were *not* encouraged to feel worthwhile.

2. Kids need to feel important.

Every time you make a choice regarding your kids, you send a message. You can't make it to a game? Your kids think it must not be important to you. Don't have time for the concert? It probably doesn't matter much to you.

Just the opposite happens when you do make the effort. How many times have you heard an adult talking about the impression made by a mom or dad who never missed a game, always came to the concerts, or always had *time*. Those are lasting impressions that will make a lifelong difference in who your kids become.

With our three boys, ballgames were important. Stu and I sat through hundreds and hundreds of tennis matches, basketball games, soccer matches, and football games. In one season alone, we attended 82 basketball games.

Out of curiosity, I decided to go back and calculate just how many games we went to now that Ryan, our youngest, has graduated from high school. I guessed the number would be between 750 and 1,000. I was surprised to see that the actual grand total went over 1,800 games, not including all the out-of-state and out-of-country events during their college days. You could say we have been enthusiastic fans of our boys.

How we spend our time—with or without them—speaks loudly and clearly. Every time we make a sacrifice, it's remembered.

One friend remembers how his mother sat up all night, patiently holding two of his teeth in place that his brother had removed rather unceremoniously while they were wrestling.

When they were able to get to a dentist the next morning, they learned that if not for her loving attention, the teeth would have been lost. Instead, even after all these years, every morning when he looks in the mirror to brush his two front teeth, he remembers his mother's love and devotion.

You never know exactly what will register with boys; mine remember French toast. For some reason, my making French toast for breakfast on game days using real French bread seemed like a sacrifice and spoke volumes to them. It has become a family memory.

Affirmation of any kind lingers long after the event. It fosters a sense of importance and self-confidence. It enhances healthy self-esteem and emotional security.

A neighbor of ours returned to teaching in an elementary school after an 11-year absence being a mom. "What's the biggest change you see after so many years away?" I asked.

Without hesitation, she answered, "The emotional insecurity of the kids."

Many parents are so busy that the kids aren't sure where they fit in their parents' hectic schedules or list of priorities. The pace, the demands, the divorce all around them, day care, always being on the run—it's overwhelming. Children need a haven, a quiet, safe, comfortable setting where they can make mistakes without ridicule, try without competition, enjoy a relaxed pace, and get special attention.

Our area has a lot of nurseries where shrubs and trees are grown for landscaping. Each nurseryman has greenhouses where the cuttings are first planted and grown. The protected environment doesn't make the plants weak and unhealthy. Just the opposite. The nurseryman knows the young cuttings need the protected environment so they can grow a strong root structure and get a healthy start. Then when they're placed out in the real world, they thrive.

Too many children today are struggling with emotional insecurity because their parents don't realize how important that

Every time you
become involved
in the daily routine
and needs of your
children, you send
the message,
"I care about you."

safe haven is. "Put them in day care," many people say. "It'll be good for them. Those folks are trained. It'll give the kids a head start in school."

Day care isn't so much the problem as is expecting day care to do the job of coloring in the lines of our kids' lives so they develop feelings of acceptance, importance, and self-esteem. It's expecting that the root structure will just grow automatically so they'll be strong and thrive in the real world. But that approach isn't working, and the evidence is seen in every elementary school.

Whenever there are strangers and peers, there will be competition—for recognition, for approval, for acceptance, for importance. And there will be winners and losers. Every kid needs to begin in a setting where there are no losers, only very important little individuals.

3. Kids need to feel cared for.

Something as simple as a routine can contribute to a child's sense of well-being. Clean clothes say "I care." Food in the refrigerator says it. Good meals say it—real meals spreading aromas through the house, not a constant diet of cardboard-wrapped real meal deals gobbled down on the run. Help with homework or chores says it. Tuning in to their hearts at bedtime speaks it loud and clear, as we saw in our home even through the boys' high-school years.

Like your kids, all my children like and dislike different foods. And they enjoyed knowing that Mom cared what did and didn't go in their lunches and what she cooked for dinners. To boys especially, enough of the right foods speaks volumes about being cared for.

We've got to have a high-touch approach to our kids' lives rather than so much high-tech thinking. They need many emotional touches during a day to be assured of our care, times when we listen, give guidance, draw lines, lend assistance, empathize, show support, and just participate in their world.

The ways you do all those things, Mom, can take many forms. Use your creativity while looking for even more ways than you use now to make a difference in your children's lives. Every time you do become involved in the daily routine and needs of your children, you send the message, "I care about you." When you make continual sacrifices to meet your children's needs, you speak volumes of the same message. And your care feels so much better and meets deeper needs than the care of a paid sitter ever could.

Being available is one of the most important ways to make someone feel cared for. A friend still remembers the pain of not being available to her child at a critical time. She was working and couldn't be located when her son was badly injured at recess—he lost three teeth and suffered a fractured jaw. What did he need more than anything? The security of having his mother there to help him face his pain. What could substitute for her? Nothing.

And don't fool yourself, Mom. Nothing can substitute for you, either. When bad things happen to your children, you're the most important person in the world, and being available is the most important job in the world you can have.

How is it, then, that otherwise-intelligent parents feel they're showing their kids they love them when they constantly send messages to the contrary? They're too busy for their kids, too heavily scheduled, too stressed, or too tired to be interested. Or they have other things to do that are just too important to take time for the "little things." But little things add up.

How would you feel about someone who *said* you were important but didn't *act* like it? "I love you, but I don't have time for what's important to you" is a very confusing message.

4. Kids need to develop good attitudes.

Our best efforts are needed to teach our children good attitudes. As your children grow up in your home, watching your example, what kinds of attitudes are they developing toward relationships, for instance? Are they viewing marriage as a positive commitment? Or are they becoming leery of entrusting themselves to a spouse? Are they learning to commit themselves to someone, to accept others unconditionally, to think the best?

When kids have good attitudes, good actions usually follow. If you have trouble with bad actions in your home, don't just discipline the actions; get to the root of the attitudes. And remember, attitudes are more caught than taught. What attitudes do you model when it comes to work, chores, caring for the family, sacrificing for others, authority, civil leaders, taxes, and your neighbors? Before you condemn your kids' attitudes, make sure you've examined the example you're modeling.

5. Kids need to develop good responses.

How we respond to the crises, threats, and inconveniences that come our way shows our kids the real us dealing with the real world. And every example we give them helps determine how they will respond to their own real world.

One time when our boys were little, we decided to earn extra money for something special. So we rose at dawn and drove to nearby berry fields to join the migrant workers harvesting the crop. After working about 30 minutes, we were approached by the foreman, who yelled at me as he wagged a long finger, "Get out of here, lady! We don't ever want to see you and those kids again!"

I was crushed, embarrassed, and insulted. I had no idea what we'd done wrong. I gathered the boys, set down our berries, and quietly started for the car. A moment later, the foreman came running up to us. He had mistaken us for another family that had caused trouble, he said. Now he apologized profusely and begged us to return. Because of our calm, respectful response, it became obvious we weren't the guilty party he had mistaken us for. Our kids took it all in.

Injustice comes in many ways. Kent made a shot to win his district singles tennis championship in a high-school tournament, and the umpire made the call in his favor. But the opponent and his coach harassed the official and intimidated him until the call was reversed. The fans were shocked. The opponent prevailed. Kent lost the match.

Kent's response was measured and noble. He was able to react well in the midst of the injustice and disappointment because his security didn't rest in that trophy. He had a healthy self-image, and his response to such an event had been formed in his nature long before the crisis. What showed on the outside was a reflection of what dwelt on the inside.

6. Kids need to develop good patterns.

Kids watch, listen, and question all we do in determining their own patterns and philosophies of life. They establish their work ethic from how we work. They learn priorities from how we spend our time and resources. They respond to or reject God based on how we live out our faith.

They watch how we handle everything, first to determine their own beliefs, and later to question them to see if they're valid. The poem below captures beautifully just how big a difference we make in our kids' lives.

Children Learn What They Live

If a child lives with criticism,
    he learns to condemn.
If a child lives with hostility,
    he learns to fight.
If a child lives with ridicule,
    he learns to be shy.
If a child lives with shame,
    he learns to be guilty.
If a child lives with tolerance,
    he learns to be patient.
If a child lives with encouragement,
    he learns confidence.

If a child lives with praise,
    he learns to appreciate.
If a child lives with fairness,
    he learns justice.
If a child lives with security,
    he learns to have faith.
If a child lives with approval,
    he learns to like himself.
If a child lives with acceptance and friendship,
    he learns to find love in the world.

                    —Dorothy Law Nolte[5]

Mom, you and I do make a difference. Moment by moment, as our children live and learn under our care, we influence the colors that add depth and richness to their lives. Our coloring greatly affects the final picture. Imagine the incredible difference you can make in your children's lives! Now, isn't that exciting?

5

Oh, They'll
Turn Out
All Right...
Won't They?

*adly, no magic formulas can guarantee our children's* future happiness. We can mother well and they may still make poor choices or meet unfortunate circumstances. But there are some basic, common-sense approaches that greatly improve the odds in favor of our kids' turning out well.

One time when Ryan was young, I planned a family dinner party for his birthday. We have a large extended family, so I've always been glad that our dining room table can accept five leaves. After cleaning the house and starting the meal, I stretched the table to its full length, set all the leaves in place, and hurried on with other preparations.

Before long, I heard a crash. There in the dining room lay my beautiful, broken table. The extension rails had snapped under the weight of the leaves, and it had all collapsed in a heap on the floor.

I had a birthday dinner to serve, and now I had no table to serve it on.

In my haste and distraction with other things, I had forgotten to add the fifth leg that was needed to support the center section whenever leaves were added. My intentions for the day had been excellent. I had a lot of other important things to attend to for the good of the whole family. But that was no excuse. If I hadn't been so distracted, my common sense would have told me extra support was needed. That's how the table was designed.

But I was in such a hurry that I just didn't think about the consequences. As I often say, if I'd just gotten "smart enough soon enough," I would have recognized the danger and taken steps to prevent it. And similarly, that's what we moms must do as well—foresee dangers for our kids and take action to prevent the trouble. It's not all that different from maintaining our cars or eating a good diet. It's called preventive maintenance, and it's critical.

In 1990, Ann Landers's daily column presented the American Medical Association's chilling report on violence, injury, and substance abuse among the nation's youth. The statistics were overwhelming. But what struck me most was the conclusion: *"Parents need to wake up and pay more attention to their children"*[1] (emphasis added).

Has parenting become such a low priority in our society that we actually need to be reminded by the American Medical Association to pay attention to our kids? Evidently so. Isn't that amazing? Isn't that sad?

Why aren't we more attuned to preventing the behavioral problems dominating our society? We're plagued with increasing problems, some of which barely existed when we were growing up. Anger, crime, violence. Drugs, sexual perversion and promiscuity, mental disorders. Defiance and rebellion. Phobias, eating disorders, teen pregnancy and abortions. Our kids are being overwhelmed. Natural coping mechanisms or instincts seem insufficient for all they face today. What in the world are we to do?

The answer is almost too easy to believe. It's so obvious, it's overlooked. The answer is in their *hearts* and *spirits*, and the home is where the remedies are worked in and the results are first lived out.

Moms, we can *hope* our kids turn out all right and don't become statistics . . . or we can *do* something about it, something to prevent trouble.

Our kids need our acceptance and attention, enough attention that we pick up on what hurts, intimidates, and tempts them. We can't get that just by sharing a kitchen and bath with

Our kids need our
acceptance and
attention, enough
attention that we
pick up on what
hurts, intimidates,
and tempts them.

them, and we can't leave encouragement and unconditional love in a note on the refrigerator. We have to share time, experiences, and our hearts.

If our kids get the acceptance from us that they so desperately need, they won't go looking for it elsewhere. And kids do need acceptance. They need identity—self-identity, not just (in our case) being "one of the Weber boys." They're looking for affirmation of what they say, how they dress, their opinions, and their mannerisms.

Kids must have affirmation or they won't grow to healthy adulthood.

Children probably fear two things more than anything else—isolation and rejection. If we leave them alone, they'll go seeking the company of someone else. If we reject them, they'll look for a place to be accepted. And it won't matter how bad the place is. It won't matter how poor the morals. Any place can feel like a haven if isolation and rejection are dispelled.

Kids need their own space, but they don't want to feel lonely or isolated. We have to watch out for the difference. We have to be careful not to barge into their space, but we also have to make sure they know we're there and available if they need us. If loneliness does start to set in, knowing we're there for them may be all the comfort they need.

And then there's rejection. We all remember rejection, don't we? When someone pointed out our mistake, commented on our hair or clothing, laughed at something we thought was embarrassing?

We all hate to be embarrassed. So why is it we so frequently embarrass our kids and then chide them for being too sensitive when they groan, "Mom!"

We can make our kids feel rejected in so many ways. After all, they're still trying to determine who they are and what they believe. Any remarks and attitudes toward their words or actions can be interpreted as a rejection of *them*, not what they're doing. We need to be sensitive to that and make sure our impact on them is positive, not negative.

Rejection can be sensed in our tone of voice, our body language, that certain look. Kids may feel rejected when we can't afford time to be with them or the money to provide something they think is important (especially if they see money going in a lot of other directions for *our* pleasures).

In addition to affirmation, children need guidance. Why do kids have sex at such early ages? Their curiosity outweighs their instruction. So let's instruct them.

Why do kids fall into substance abuse? They don't know all the dangers. So let's educate them. They don't have the self-confidence to say no. So let's build up their sense of identity. They need acceptance, and they'll do some of the dumbest things to get it. So let's shower them with acceptance.

Moms, we have to get smart enough soon enough. We may wait until we've been robbed to install an alarm system because, "Well, I didn't want to waste the money if we didn't have the need." But we can't take that approach with our kids. We have to take preventive measures all along the way.

Why wait until we see them out with the wrong crowd? Why wait until we sense things aren't all that healthy with the boyfriend or girlfriend? Why wait until they become secretive or avoid us?

Instead, let's anticipate some of the problems, have our antennae up, and show we're on their side. Let's communicate, discussing the difficult issues kids face while they're still theory. Let's make sure we're both available and approachable. Let's not wait until we see red flags before we begin to develop a plan. Preventing negative experiences requires positive planning.

I remember clearly a time when Stu and I had to take preventive steps with our son Blake. When he was 13 or so, a boy named Dan on his soccer team really took to Blake; he almost seemed to worship him. Blake, in turn, was drawn to Dan.

The phone rang regularly as the two buddies stayed in constant touch. Whenever there was an event to attend, a game to see, or just an urge to go out and do something, those boys wanted to be together. It's great to have friends, isn't it?

From my perspective, however, Dan had an attitude problem. He didn't respond well to any authority—parents, teachers, coaches, even suggestions from friends. He often kept information from his parents. And his language was laced with profanity.

In addition, Dan's family was seldom home. (Do you see any connection?) Both parents worked long hours, so he received little supervision and had virtually no boundaries placed around him. As a result, he was trouble waiting to happen, and when it did, I didn't want Blake anywhere near it.

To put it bluntly, I was uncomfortable with Dan's being Blake's best friend, because I knew that especially with teens, peer influence is strong. Already I was seeing a new defensiveness developing in Blake. He would make excuses for Dan, who seemingly could do no wrong in his eyes. And he wouldn't listen to any of our concerns about Dan's attitude and actions.

Because of that negative effect on Blake's personality and loyalties, Stu and I decided we had no choice but to step in. We warned Blake of the tendencies we saw growing, and we said that rather than help build his life and character, Dan was actually serving to tear them down. Though we didn't forbid Blake to see Dan, we did ask him to phase out gradually his close friendship with Dan and to start doing more with other buddies.

Blake listened, but he wasn't very receptive to our point of view. Nonetheless, because of the solid relationship of mutual respect that we had built with him over the years, little by little he started seeking out other friends to fill his free time. He didn't like our request, but he chose to honor our desires.

In the years that followed, the two boys went down different roads. Dan, unfortunately, chose a path of drugs, alcohol, and disposable relationships. And today, when Blake looks back at that friendship, he understands why we acted as we did. Not long ago, something brought Dan to his mind, and he told us, "Thanks, Mom and Dad, for steering me when I couldn't see the potholes in the road."

Mom, let's be sure we're providing the right atmosphere in our homes, making them places that encourage good things and help bad things dissolve before they can get a foothold. Let's be careful to watch what's going on. Let's be backers instead of critics, and we'll see the daily crises lose momentum and fall away.

To dispel the negative things in life, we need to add a lot to the positive side. Let's have fun with our kids. Let's show them that we enjoy them. Let's make our times together happy times. Let's live our moments with them to the fullest.

Remember, Mom, make your home a happy place to be, not just a stopover between events. When your kids face the dark moments of growing up, they'll run to the one place where they feel secure and accepted. Let's make sure that's home.

6

What Is Nurturing, Anyway?

"*M*ommy!"

Can't you just hear your children calling to you from another room? What a precious sound that was in my ear all the years one of our little guys was roaming around our house!

He probably didn't need much of anything, just the assurance that I was close by; maybe a chance to chatter about his favorite toy or what he was going to do when Grampa came to visit. But what a pleasant memory for me, hearing my little guys call out over the years, "Mommy!" I wouldn't trade it for the world. And I wouldn't trade the time together, the unhurried seasons when I didn't have to worry about the clock, about making it to appointments or fitting my mothering into a crowded schedule. I don't miss the things we did without. Instead, I have the moments we shared, and those are treasures in my heart that will never wear out or fade away. You see, we decided early on that spending time together was much more important than accumulating things. So we used what money we had more on shared experiences than on collecting objects for the house or garage. And I wouldn't trade that decision for anything.

Some people might tell me I could have accomplished more if I had been working instead of just staying home. That's because they don't understand that I was doing far more than cleaning house and making peanut butter sandwiches. I was being available, approachable, tuned in. I was nurturing. And in my case, I felt as though I did that best by staying home. The same might not be true of you. We'll discuss that more in chapter 10.

What is nurturing? My dictionary defines it with words like *nourishing, sustaining, supporting, feeding, fostering, cherishing, educating, training,* and *rearing.* That sounds like a pretty good calling to me. I certainly can't think of any of those things that I'd be willing for my boys to do without. They all make such lasting differences throughout a child's life.

Nurturing is essential. None of us can be deprived of it without being permanently affected.

Not long ago, Stu and I were in Palm Springs attending a seminar. We were having dinner in a nice restaurant when two older women sat down at a table near us. Though their dress and manners portrayed women very much "together" and in control, one of them was obviously distressed. Because of our proximity and the loudness of her voice, we heard her pour out her heart to her friend.

Though at least 65, she still suffered the pain and rejection of her childhood. Her mother hadn't been at home much when this lady was growing up. When she *was* home, she had little time for her daughter. The girl was pretty much left on her own, given the responsibilities a mother usually would have assumed.

The woman still resented her mom for always being gone. She still resented her mother's work, because it seemed it was always more important than her. And she still resented the lack of time spent together. It seemed to her as if her mother never taught her anything, not even a simple thing like how to cook, much less how to live.

She still suffered strong feelings of abandonment, hurt, and confusion. Even decades later, she was talking about her depression over that lack and the poor self-image it had generated.

Isn't that sad? A woman in her sixties had to try to resolve her childhood pain, knowing her relationships today are still heavily affected by that vital early relationship. Why? All because as a little girl, she never felt nurtured by her mother. She made no mention or complaint of conditions—wealth or poverty. (And though those are rarely the heart of any issue, today many of us race to make more and have more, as if that would solve every need and ensure our family's emotional health and happiness.)

All those problems after all those years, still haunting that dear woman because her mother wasn't there for her.

Robert Lewis and William Hendricks write of an even-more-tragic example. A young man seemingly had all the advantages in the world. He came from a famous and well-to-do family. He had graduated at the top of his class from one of the most highly regarded universities. He was a successful businessman with a wife and family. And yet all that was overshadowed by his great unmet needs from childhood.

> In 1949, actress Mercedes McCambridge won an Academy Award. I'm sure she felt on top of the world. Certainly she was at the top of her career. The whole industry applauded what she had accomplished on film.
>
> But her son, John, didn't join the party. To the outside world, the McCambridge home glittered. But for a son who needed a mother, this family was anything but a success. Even though John later became a very successful financial broker, his life was haunted by the deficits his upbringing had left within him. In the spring of 1989, he exploded. Before murdering his own wife and two children and then committing suicide, he penned these words to his famous mother:[1]
>
> "I was essentially raised by live-in maids and relatives. You never were there for me. I tried to get your love through academic achievement, gifts, and, finally, enormous personal risk. You love to tell the story of the boy who got paid to babysit himself. That means I was left alone. Alone! At five years

old, in his little suit and hat, flying across the country alone. Alone! Is this clear to you, mom? . . . There is nothing more to say."[2]

Lewis concluded his story with this:

You will leave in your children what you have lived out in your home. Can you imagine the horror and heartbreak that this young man's mother must have felt? Yet his tragic outcome was forged long ago. His wings were clipped long before he got married. Though highly gifted with intelligence, he obviously grew up without emotional stability.[3]

What does all that tell you? We can't nurture from a distance. And nurturing is built around our availability and wise understanding of each child's personality and needs, not the things we provide.

To build a strong house, you begin with a solid foundation. If the foundation has flaws—breaks in the undergirding—the whole house will be unstable regardless of how it looks from the outside.

Because the foundation our lives are built upon is so important, many approaches to counseling rely heavily on learning about the foundation—the "family of origin." How the father and mother lived, and how they related to one another and to their children, give tremendous insights into why children approach and live out their lives the way they do. Cracks in the walls usually mean faults in the foundation. Just think, our children might be talking to counselors someday about what we did right or wrong as parents.

From the very beginning, Mom, you play an invaluable role in your children's growth and development. Your nurturing builds that foundation. It might not be instantly measurable, but don't dismiss your critical importance. The foundation you lay will be much more important than anything else you could

When children feel good about life and themselves, good behavior usually results, and they enjoy healthy approaches to dealing with life.

ever produce or purchase for that child.

Think about it for a moment. When you go shopping, can you follow the theory that "if it looks good, it is good"? Would you buy melons that way? Would you rely on the packaging to tell you if a product is sound? Of course not. What you see on the outside often isn't a good indication of content. And the same is true with raising children.

There are the "seen" aspects of mothering—making sure your child is bathed, well-fed, rested, and sheltered. All those are extremely important, but they're insufficient by themselves. There are also the "unseen" aspects—the learning and equipping we're providing, the atmosphere we set that stimulates good feelings, a sense of security and acceptance, and self-worth.

Our children come into the world helpless, needing our care and attention to their physical needs. But they also come with emotional needs, and as they grow and their hearts are wounded, they'll be more needy at some times than at others. That's why our understanding of their unique, individual needs and our availability is so important. That's why nurturing comes with proximity. How can it occur at a distance or in our absence?

When you read of crimes and violence in your newspaper, have you ever stopped to think about how many of those acts could probably be traced to what life was like for those individuals when they were children? And when you read some uplifting story where a child has overcome great odds to be successful, what's always behind it? Someone nurturing, giving the child the sense of security and self-confidence to set out and do something worthwhile because he believes he *is* worthwhile.

When children feel good about life and themselves, good behavior usually results, and they enjoy healthy approaches to dealing with life. When children feel bad about life or themselves, bad behavior results, and with it comes inner turmoil—anger, resentment, and distrust, all unhealthy ways of coping with life.

So when we're there, nurturing our children, mending wounded hearts, providing that atmosphere that stimulates healthy growth, we're making a lasting contribution to our children's lives.

It seems like just a few months ago that all our boys were home. What a whirlwind of energy and activity! And now, at the time of this writing, Kent is in graduate school, Blake is graduating from college, and Ryan is graduating from high school. To a large extent, that window of time we had to shape their lives is closing. My little nest is emptying out, and I don't know what I'd do if I didn't have the assurance that I gave it all I had when my opportunity was there.

Don't let your window of opportunity go by without making the most of it, Mom. The time will pass faster than you can imagine.

Some moms may think nurturing really isn't too important right now. After all, the baby is so young, it won't matter if Mom's busy doing "more important" or "more fulfilling" things. Others whose kids are a little older may think they look pretty well-grounded, that they're past the nurturing stage.

You might be surprised.

In Brenda Hunter's excellent book *Home By Choice*, she shows the impact of separation when a mom leaves a child:

> As Erik Larson wrote in *Parents* magazine:
> "Separation is serious business, and psychologists now conduct their research with increasing urgency. They cite the large numbers of children who must cope with separation as their moms go back to work and as divorce breaks up more families."
> When Ricky's mother, Eva, initially left him in

the neighborhood day care center, he sobbed as she walked out the door. Over the next four years, Ricky, who told his parents that he didn't like going to day care, ceased to show any emotion when his mother dropped him off and collected him at day's end. Throughout his childhood Ricky spent most of his waking hours at Wee People, and his sister, Janice, who had entered elementary school, spent her late afternoons there as well.

One day a clinical psychologist came to the center to get Janice to play with her daughter. As Janice put on her coat and said goodbye to Ricky, the psychologist noticed that though tears flowed down Ricky's cheeks, the little boy stood mutely by. He didn't even ask to accompany his sister on the outing.

This psychologist who works with troubled adolescents later told a colleague about this episode, saying that Ricky had already learned his efforts made little difference in his world. "Someday he may become a depressed teenager," she said, "and not know why. He will be suffering from 'learned helplessness,' having discovered early on that his crying, his attempts to bring his mother back, didn't work."[4]

Is it just a matter of timing, waiting until they're a little older before we jump back onto the career path? Here's what my friend Ann told me:

For the first nine years of my life, Mom stayed home. She spent time playing, teaching, and caring for my brother, sister, and me. She was a room mother at my school and a Girl Scout leader. Those days felt so good. I knew Mom would be there when I needed her. I was her helper, and I felt important.

But when I was ten, Mom went to work full-time. I still wanted to be her helper; I wanted to feel important. So I began to take on the role of being the mom myself. I made sure the house was picked up. I often made dinner. I tried to tell my brother and sister what to do. And I knew Mom always came home tired, so I tried to make things pleasant for her. Her praise was my reward.

It's good for kids to help out. But maybe if Mom hadn't worked, I would have spent more time with friends my own age doing what kids do. I definitely would have spent less time as a little housewife. And maybe I would have learned that my significance should be based on who I am, not what I do.

Ann's mom started well. She just turned from nurturing to working outside the home too soon and forgot about giving attention to her children's special needs. Doing so has had lasting effects. Working wasn't the problem; her becoming sidetracked without realizing it was. And sometimes when we veer off course, it derails others as well. But we may not see the result until we look in the rearview mirror after it's too late.

Mom, listen carefully. This is so important. Nurturing is a continual process. It's both a process of maintaining the foundation blocks that have been laid and building on them as well. Where nurturing at a particular point in life is missing, there will be gaps in the foundation. And with those gaps will be weaknesses in self-concept and sense of security.

As I grew up in an apple orchard in central Washington, I saw good examples of what nurturing is all about. It's an ongoing process. You don't plant an orchard and then say, "Mission accomplished. Time to relax." And you don't raise confident kids that way, either.

Being orchard growers would be hard for some of us, because it's hard to wait for results. But that's the way apple growing works. There are few immediate results and rewards. It takes patience and diligence. And it takes confidence that the harvest is coming. That's the way nurturing works, too. Nurturing is a combination of time and attention. If the formula doesn't have both ingredients, or if they're not properly balanced, nurturing doesn't happen.

When a new section of orchard was planted, the young trees were carefully dug in and staked. A ground cover was planted between the rows to be tilled in later to provide nutrients for the roots. And in our dry climate, irrigation was used extensively. The trees were set in good soil and provided with the support and nutrition needed to ensure their growth.

The same approach applies to our kids. It's critical that we place them in an environment where they're provided with the right support and protection and given an environment where they can begin to grow without feeling trampled, overshadowed, or overlooked.

That's why I'm so concerned about the increasing numbers of mothers turning their children over to day care while they pursue careers or the accumulation of things. I don't resent the day-care providers, but I am concerned about the inevitable impact of the day-care environment and the potential effects laid out in chapter 8.

A tree grower doesn't just hope there's enough nourishment available for his trees to flourish. By his efforts, he *ensures* it. Our kids need to have their innermost beings nourished and refreshed as much as they need their bodies fed to ensure growth. Can we take any more casual approach to meeting their needs than the farmer does to meeting the needs of his trees?

Even as the trees begin to bear fruit, their young branches

Encouraging
healthy growth isn't
just a matter of
proper launching,
but also of staying
alongside, walking
with, keeping close.

are often too fragile to bear all the weight and must be propped up and supported. The same is true of our children. When their loads get too heavy for them to bear alone, we need to prop them up and support them. To do that, we have to be there and be aware. Encouraging healthy growth isn't just a matter of proper launching, but also of staying alongside, walking with, keeping close.

I remember how one of our sons had an especially hard time in junior high school. His main teacher one year didn't seem to like him or much of anything he did. That discouraged him constantly. His athletic efforts weren't very successful that year, either, which further darkened his outlook. He was always down on himself and resolved to quit more than once.

His little branches of self-esteem were too fragile to bear the weight of this period alone, so I vowed to give an extra measure of myself to him. Even though he refuted my compliments and ignored my praise, I worked hard to be positive and keep finding right things he was doing that I could applaud. I constantly told him how wonderful and special he was, and that I knew he could make it.

It took a couple of years to get him out of that slump. The extra effort was exhausting and frustrating. Yet I'm convinced that if I hadn't determined to prop him up at that point, his life could easily have taken a lasting negative turn.

Isn't that what mothering is all about? Doesn't it feel right that we were made to be the nurturers? Our husbands are wired differently. They're made more to conquer, to accomplish, to overcome. Their challenges often bring more measurable responses and immediate results. Our children will grow best as we each live out what we were best designed for.

Moms, we're the ones who create the climate, the security, the safety zone. We're the ones who provide the steady support and encouragement.

An absentee orchard grower wouldn't be very effective. He couldn't just schedule routine maintenance without being there to inspect the trees and evaluate their needs. He couldn't simply leave orders to set out smudge pots on a certain date to avoid frosts. And he couldn't choose the day to begin harvesting based on an almanac. Without being there and being aware, he'd never have much hope of reaping a good harvest.

Why, then, are so many absentee parents convinced they can automatically "schedule maintenance" for their kids to ensure all their needs are met? The right kind of toy, the right sports club, or the right extracurricular activities won't ensure well-balanced, healthy kids. More has to be introduced into young lives than supervised competition to stimulate real growth and maturity.

If kids are always in a group setting, where does individual pruning take place? Individual encouragement? Individual correction? And if there's no time for nurturing, how do we expect our kids to become all they can be?

I like the way my friend Rebecca approaches mothering:

> I enjoy flowers very much. When my children were little, I likened them to flowers. Geraniums, for instance, can endure hot temperatures and direct sunlight. In fact, that's what it takes for them to produce their brilliant blossoms. Others, like impatiens, require constant shade. Direct sunlight is detrimental. Their blooms can be just as vibrant as the geraniums when they're allowed to grow where they're intended to grow.
>
> The same is true of our children. I'm convinced the best thing we can do for our children in their early years is to be in constant study and observation of them—not to scrutinize their behavior constantly, but to learn, both for our own sake and for theirs.
>
> When I put new flowers into the garden, I also put some ugly hedge around them to prevent the

slugs from getting at them. That's a lot of work, and quite frankly, the hedge isn't pretty. But it's needed. The same is true of our kids. Are we providing a "hedge" around them to prevent damage from outside sources so their root systems can take hold and one day they can stand on their own? Nurturing mothers try to protect their children from all the things that harm them, not only physically, but mentally and emotionally as well—not to make them weak, but to allow them a good start to grow strong.

How Jason reacts to a situation is totally different from Tim's reaction. Some things matter a lot more to Emily than they do to either of the boys. The kids are the healthiest, and we have the best relationships with them, when we understand what's important to each one and what intimidates each one.

Gary and I thoroughly enjoy our children. Is it because they're exceptional? I don't think so. I think it's because we've tried to be good students of our children.

What is nurturing? It's protecting, feeding, encouraging. It's strengthening, building, developing, establishing. Most of all, remember that nurturing *is a continual process* requiring time, attention, discernment, and great care.

Mom, no investment you make in life will yield the returns you'll get from nurturing your children. So enjoy your role, and be encouraged by the importance of doing it well.

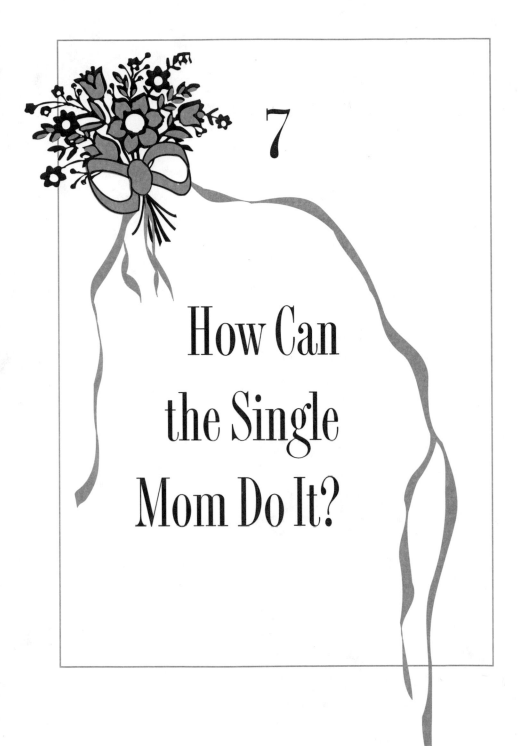

7

How Can the Single Mom Do It?

*ore and more moms are finding themselves left* without a spouse and handed *all* the responsibility of raising a family. A recent news report stated that the number of single-parent households has actually doubled in just the last 20 years. For most single mothers, that means working a job full-time and parenting full-time. That's quite a load, to say the least.

From watching my single mother as I was growing up, and from witnessing the lives of many women who are in that situation now, four things stand out as essentials if you're going to succeed, not just survive, as a single mom.

1. Strive to have a positive attitude.

Attitude is everything. It affects both mental and physical health, and it largely determines whether you succeed or fail. People who think they can, usually can. People who don't think they can, usually can't—whatever the issue at hand, whatever the demand. You must have a positive attitude if you want to succeed.

But single moms can become weighed down with emotions that are like strikes against them when it comes to choosing their attitude.

One strike can be anger. Anger because they're alone. Anger toward their ex-husband. Anger because the world isn't fair. Anger because they have to struggle at a job and then go home and be both a mom and a dad to their children. Anger because people just don't understand the unrelenting demands that pull at them day in and day out, all week and all weekend.

When anger is unresolved, it causes damage inside and out.

A second strike may be resentment. Unresolved anger can become resentment toward others. Very often it's misdirected and becomes aimed at parents, friends, or churches who may not have had a role in events or any power to sway them. Resentment hurts both the person who feels it and those around her.

If resentment isn't dealt with, it can turn inward and fester into bitterness. *Fester* is such an appropriate word. It's not used much anymore, but there was a time when any mother knew what festering was. Until recent improvements in medicines and sanitation, most people knew about boils. A boil is a painful, localized, pus-filled swelling of the skin. It's caused by a bacterial infection.

There's no real home treatment for a boil until it has formed a head—a channel to the skin's surface that eventually allows the pus to be drained off. When that appears, the wound can be lanced, drained, and cleaned. Then the swelling will go down and the boil can heal. If not drained, a boil will continue to generate pus, increasing the swelling, the pressure, and the pain. And the infection will spread, forming new boils.

Sometimes we feel as if we *deserve* to carry around bitter feelings. Letting go can feel like saying, "It really doesn't matter so much." But we feel just the opposite. It *does* matter so much. And it *hurts* so much. But not dealing with anger and resentment is like covering a boil, hoping it will simply go away. It won't. It will only fester, grow, spread, and erupt in other places. And the pain will only increase.

You don't really *deserve* to carry around your anger and bitterness. You *deserve* to be free of it. Letting it go doesn't mean it didn't matter. It just means it isn't worth the cost of hanging on to the infection. Striving to have a positive attitude is like sunshine and fresh air. It's cleansing. It lightens your load. It strengthens and renews health. That's what you really deserve.

If you're locked up with bad feelings and damaged emotions

and feel you can't move on, look for help. Almost always, unresolved issues will paralyze you emotionally. You need a source outside yourself to help you deal with those roadblocks, to sort them out, and to move beyond them. Smart people get help. Be smart. Go to a close friend you can trust. Go to a pastor. Find a counselor. But get help.

Seeking the guidance of others isn't a show of weakness. It isn't just the latest approach in pop psychology. Such a wise approach to life has been known throughout the centuries. The biblical book of Proverbs says, "Where there is no guidance, the people fall, but in abundance of counselors there is victory."[1]

With a positive attitude, you can take whatever situation you're in and make the most of it. It will be your greatest weapon in fighting despair. You can do it; you just have to *believe* you can.

Often it's not the circumstances so much as your view of them that needs the adjustment. Ruth Bell Graham tells a story of some fishermen in Scotland who gathered at an inn to rest and enjoy a cup of hot tea.

> Just as the waitress was serving them, one of the men began describing the day's catch in typical fisherman gestures, and his right hand collided with a tea cup. The contents splashed all over the whitewashed wall and an ugly brown stain emerged.
>
> "I'm so terribly sorry," the fisherman apologized repeatedly.
>
> "Never mind," said a man who jumped up from a nearby table. Pulling a crayon from his pocket, he began to sketch around the tea stain, and there emerged a magnificent royal stag with his antlers spread. The artist was Sir Edwin Henry Landseer, England's foremost painter of animals.
>
> If an artist can do that with an ugly brown stain,

what can God do with my sins and my mistakes if I
give them over to Him?[2]

Julie is a young, single mom and the sweetest person you
could ever meet. You look at her and think, *The husband who
abandoned her should have his head examined. She didn't
deserve that.*

When her husband first left, Julie was overwhelmed with
grief and the responsibility of caring for her two early-teen children alone. She struggled with feelings of rejection, fear, and
devastation.

Her turning point toward renewed health and successful living came, she says, when she decided to lay aside her anger
and despair and take positive responsibility for providing a
secure home for her children. She knew it wouldn't be easy,
but she was determined to do the job and do it well.

Julie realized she couldn't do the job alone, however, so she
got involved with a support group through her church. From
other members she learned coping skills and gained understanding help. For her emotional health, she went to counseling and took classes. She even got training to help other
women in the same situation.

It was difficult for Julie to quit blaming her former husband
for her struggles and take this kind of responsibility. It required
some heavy-duty anger resolution. But in the process, she
became free to enjoy life again.

Julie works hard to provide a healthy environment for her
kids, being there for them when she's not at her job, making
financial sacrifices to give them opportunities for development—and all with a positive outlook on life. She has also
found mentors to give them a constant, healthy male presence.
She made the kids' daytime caregiver a friend of the family so
she's not just "the sitter." And for the children's sake, she has
tried to maintain as good a relationship as possible with their
father.

Julie's life as a single mom takes extra effort day after day. But with determination and a positive attitude, she's making it.

The same can be true for you. Take heart. Strive to have a positive attitude. Get help in doing that if you need it. But begin to look at your situation in a different light, and make something of it that will count.

2. Refuse to give in to comparisons.

Comparisons can be deadly. First, they're usually shortsighted and incorrect. You never see the whole story. You don't know what other people may be dealing with. Anyway, we're each unique. None of us is alike, so why are we always comparing ourselves to one another?

When we make comparisons, we begin to have expectations. And often, those expectations are unreasonable. Just as a poor family can't expect to have a house and car as nice as those of their more-well-to-do neighbors, you can't expect to produce the same energy and creativity around the house as your married, stay-at-home friend next door. That's just not realistic. The best advice is to use your mental and physical energy determining how to make the most of your situation, not focusing on comparisons or expending all your efforts trying to match someone else's standard of living.

A friend went flying in a small plane with his son. Something happened aboard the plane that caused it to go down. Our friend, Mick, survived. His son did not. As a result of his loss, he often says, " Things wouldn't be so hard if we didn't expect them to be so easy."

Things won't be so difficult for you as a single mom if you don't expect them to be easy. Refuse to make the comparisons. Refuse to buy into the expectations of keeping up with someone else, of having everything they have. The truth is, you won't be able to do everything. You may not have all you want or once had. But that's okay. Our lives are not measured in our abundance of things.

3. Never give up.

When you give up, you quit fighting. When you quit fighting, you lose. Never give up, because only by hanging in will you win.

Determination is necessary to overcome any obstacle, any challenge, any handicap. Whenever something doesn't work out, you have to try again. Maybe from a different angle, maybe in a different way, but you have to keep trying.

I used to play tennis with June. June had only one hand, so tennis was a big challenge for her. Imagine learning to toss the ball in the air and then hit it with a racket, all using one hand. That's how she served. It wasn't easy. It took more energy than the normal way. But she never gave up, and she became an excellent player.

Another tennis partner battled cancer for ten years before she died. Even during her chemotherapy, Marci never surrendered. It was months before I learned she wore a wig, one result of her treatment. It was no big deal to her, nothing worth discussing.

She was determined not to miss a single week of tennis. One day she told me she had discovered why she had played so poorly the week before—she had a broken rib! I asked if she dared try to play again. "Oh, I'll be okay," she responded. "My ribs are taped this week." Marci simply refused to give up, and because of that, she enjoyed life despite the obstacles until the cancer finally won.

Both my friends had a plan, a focus. They set a goal in front of themselves, and they never gave up striving for it. Do the same for yourself. Set a goal, have a plan, and never give up.

4. Nurture your soul.

All of us need a resource outside ourselves. And everyone needs to go to that source for nourishment and refreshment. Nurture your soul. Refresh it. Don't neglect the needs of your innermost being.

Whenever something
doesn't work out,
you have to try again.
Maybe from a different
angle, maybe in a
different way, but you
have to keep trying.

For our family, our source has been God Himself.

Back in that little migrant shack, my mother nurtured her soul from the Bible every day. When there was no soap for the washing machine, Mom would remind us that God would provide. When things were especially hard, she would rehearse for us how good God was, how He would never leave us. When my father became abusive and she was in physical danger, she would reflect on God's promises and remind us that He knows all things. Though we had almost nothing, she would assure us we had all we needed.

Imagine the inner strength she must have had to endure those hard days. That strength remained constant because she nurtured her soul. And imagine the foundation it gave her three children. We saw what really mattered. We saw how to lay a foundation to support us against anything we would ever face in life. We learned where to go for our own inner strength. And what security and emotional stamina that built into us!

How can the single mom do it? It's not an easy road. Strive to have a positive attitude. Refuse to give in to comparisons. Never give up. And nurture your soul. For my mother, that meant reading her Bible, believing God was big enough to deal with her problems, and then choosing to live like it. I pray these will be your resolutions, too. They work!

8

What Is Quality Child Care?

his chapter on child care may well be the most challenging one in the entire book. I know I'm stepping into dangerous territory here. My friends at Focus on the Family tell me that whenever they air a broadcast or publish an article about working mothers, regardless of what they say, they get critical letters from both sides of the issue. Moms who work outside the home write, "Why are you trying to make us feel more guilty?" Stay-at-home moms write, "Why are you downplaying the importance of what we do?" It seems to be a real catch-22 subject.

Nonetheless, because I know you love your children deeply and want to be the best mom you can possibly be, and because I want to be a friend who helps you toward that goal, I'm going to venture boldly into the arena and say what I believe with all my heart. I know there are many moms reading this who have children still at home and who truly have no choice but to work outside the home. For them, it isn't just a matter of wanting to maintain a certain life-style or standard of living. But we need to discuss here the primary principle rather than focusing on exceptions to the rule of what's best for our kids. Every mother must seek God's will for her unique situation.

For most of the rest of this chapter, I'm going to give my reasons for being leery of outside child care. Our choices are only as good as the information on which we base them. We need to become properly informed so we can make decisions based on solid facts rather than allowing our society to push us in the direction of the current trend. Please read these pages in the spirit of loving concern with which they were written. And even if you have no choice but to work outside the home and leave your children in day care, please stay with me to the end, because there I will offer some suggestions for how to find the very best care available to you. (I am thankful to Dr. Brenda Hunter, in her book *Home By Choice*, for pointing me to much of the research cited in this chapter.)

For some reason, telephone poles seem to have become billboards around our community. I can stop at almost any intersection and read a number of flyers.

> Garage Sale, 8 to 5, Sat. and Sun.
> Firewood, Maple & Fir, Delivered
> Reward: Have You Seen Our Golden Retriever?
> Quality Child Care in My Home

Quality child care? From a phone number stapled to a telephone pole along Hogan Road? Is that all the recommendation needed today to consider placing children in a stranger's care? Have we become so desperate? Is child care really that much in demand?

Not long ago, I received a letter from Kendall, a young friend who works in a day-care center. It read,

> I encourage and plead with you to write your book on the value of motherhood. Working at a day-care center for the past three years has given me a stark view of where American families, especially women, are headed. Motherhood is no longer valued and is seen more as a mark of prestige than as the precious gift it truly is.
>
> The marks are deep. Now our American little girls are growing up playing office, banker, and travel agent while they take their baby dolls to a day-care center or sitter.

That was a strong statement, so I called Kendall and asked her to tell me more about her concerns. She said,

Not all mothers who bring their children to day care are bad mothers. But I see a lot of tired mothers who don't have any patience at the end of the day. I see too many of them whisk their kids off to another baby-sitter for the evening while they take care of themselves. And I see the children's personalities reflect the parents'—they're short and impatient with their friends and teachers.

When I was little, we played house. There was a mommy and a daddy. These little girls don't play house. They never cook a meal; they microwave everything. I never see them nurturing their dolls. They just put them in a crib and have their friends take care of them.

These little girls all want to be like boys. I see that a lot. They're very competitive. But they're not at all nurturing.

Kendall works in a day-care center because she loves children. She has no ax to grind with day care and no grudge to bear against mothers. She's merely reporting what she sees. And what she sees is too many mothers using child care as a substitute parent and forgetting to nurture. And she sees little girls mimicking their mommies—put the baby doll aside and get to the office.

Saddest of all, Kendall sees moms running kids from one hired sitter to another so they can get on with their own lives without the burden or inconvenience of their kids. And sometimes, the more concerned the mom is to live *her* life to the fullest, the less importance seems to be placed on decisions affecting her *child's* life.

I shudder when I read what researchers are discovering as they study children placed in child care at early ages. This research doesn't point fingers at the abilities or intentions of child-care providers. Instead, it points fingers at the effects of *parental absence.* No matter how great the caregiver, the parent is needed most.

> Babies need their mothers. They need them during their earliest years more than they need baby-sitters, toys, or the material comforts a second income will buy.[1]
>
> The evidence since 1980 indicates that when a baby is placed in substitute care, even good quality care such as nanny care, for twenty or more hours per week during his first year of life, he is at risk psychologically. If a mother returns to work during her baby's first year, there's a significant chance the child will be insecurely attached to mother and/or father.[2]

Developmental Psychology reported studies conducted by Schwarz, Strickland, and Krolick that conclude that children

> in day care from infancy . . . compared on nine behavioral traits with matched subjects who had no day care experience prior to the study were found to be significantly more aggressive, motorically active (more inclined to run about), and less cooperative with adults. . . . The infant group (day care from infancy) was also rated as more physically and verbally aggressive with peers and adults. There was a tendency for the infant group to be less tolerant of frustration. . . . The present findings suggest caution as we proceed into the day care era.[3]

Ron Haskins of the University of North Carolina at Chapel Hill did a study of children with varying amounts and types of day-care experience. These children were now being rated by school teachers in public school during their first two to three years there. "Multivariate analysis indicated that children who had attended a cognitively oriented day-care program beginning

Too much is at stake
to take shortcuts,
hope for the best,
or assume
someone else
will do a good job.

in infancy were more aggressive than all other groups of children who had attended day care." The consensus was that the early day-care children were more prone to hit, kick, push, threaten, swear, and argue.[4]

"Teachers said these early day care children did not have strategies for dealing with their angry feelings; instead of talking about how they felt or walking away, they lashed out."[5]

Freud describes the relationship of a young child to his mother as "unique, without parallel, established unalterably for a whole lifetime as the first and strongest love object and as the prototype of all later love relationships for both sexes."[6]

If that relationship is interrupted by child care substituted for the mother, the impact is immense. British psychiatrist John Bowlby states, "The young child's hunger for his mother's love and presence is as great as his hunger for food. And in consequence her absence inevitably generates a powerful sense of loss and anger."[7] Young children desperately need the emotional accessibility of a parent. That stability forms the foundation for all relationships to come.

The effect of early attachment to the mother goes far beyond just adjusting to kindergarten or the first grade. Judith Viorst says,

> When separation imperils that early attachment,
> it is difficult to build confidence, to build trust, to
> acquire the conviction that throughout the course
> of life we will—and deserve to—find others to
> meet our needs. And when our first connections
> are unreliable or broken or impaired, we may
> transfer that experience, and our responses to that
> experience, onto what we expect from our children,
> our friends, our marriage partner.[8]

A friend took her car in to have the wheels balanced. After a short wait, the workman returned, filled out the appropriate paperwork, took her payment, and told her she was ready to go. But in his haste, he'd forgotten to replace the lug nuts on one wheel. Soon after she pulled onto a freeway, the wheel came loose and rolled across several lanes of traffic, causing a multi-car accident.

Sometimes things in life look fine, but then "the wheels fall off." Too much is at stake to take shortcuts, hope for the best, or assume someone else will do a good job. Brenda Hunter tells us this: "For a child, absence does not make the heart grow fonder. Instead, absence generates profound feelings of rejection and a yearning for love that can dominate the whole of life."[9]

Child-care advocates will tell you a child naturally establishes strong bonds with a caregiver, and that's true. But that doesn't necessarily mean it's good. "A child's mind is like a video tape recorder, carefully transcribing every word, right down to the tone of voice and facial expressions. And all of it contributes to the person he will become. Some psychologists say his emotional pattern is set by the time he is two years old."[10]

And whom will the child mimic? The one with whom he spends significant waking hours. "A child needs at least one person he trusts and feels is in charge. That figure is the baby's 'touchstone' — the one he goes to when he is sick or frightened or sad. *All others are secondary.*"[11] Attachment will take place. The question is, whom do we choose to take this influential position?

Whom will your child pattern himself after? Whom will he see when he wakes? When he experiences the rushes of good feelings from being fed, changed, or bathed, who will be indelibly etched in his mind, you or a caregiver?

Others just don't have the deep concern for my child that I have. No one else is as ready to make the sacrifices, to take the time to nurture and encourage, as I am. So who could better care for my child, especially during his first years when he is so impressionable and easily molded?

Many people can carefully attend to your young child. Many people can provide quality food and supervision. But that doesn't ensure the emotional health, stability, or well-being of your little one. Mom, your child's identity will be indelibly stamped with the identity of the significant caregiver. His security and self-esteem will be permanently affected by his setting, especially if he has to establish himself in a crowd of other little folks all clamoring for attention, recognition, and regard.

You must look deeper than good food and supervision when you determine for yourself, "What is quality child care?"

The bottom line is this: If you have to use child care, use it as a supplement to your nurturing, not a substitute. Treat your search for care with as much thoroughness as you would use in searching for the best heart surgeon. Use the following three guidelines in conducting your search.

First, look for a home atmosphere, with only one or two other children present at most, rather than a large-group setting like a franchised day-care center. There's just no way kids can get the individualized attention they need in the large-group situation. The ideal situation might be to find someone who can come to your home and give your children the most secure environment of all.

Second, do a thorough examination of all potential caregivers. Interview them closely, ask for references, and question all the references as well. It's not a bad idea to ask local churches for recommendations, but that's not foolproof, either. Examine those people as carefully as any others. And only consider people with a proven record of positive experiences.

Finally, look for caregiving situations that will allow you to maximize your own involvement with your children. Perhaps you can trade baby-sitting with a friend. Or you might find a job-sharing arrangement or a part-time position that meets your financial needs but doesn't require you to leave your children with someone else a full eight hours a day. Also explore the possibility of a home-based business if you have skills that can be used that way, such as word processing or craft making. (Many resources are available to help you identify such skills and business opportunities, including Focus on the Family's book *Homemade Business,* by Donna Partow.)

Mom, you have a unique place in your child's life, and you will make a unique impact—one way or the other. Make it the best it's within your power to give.

9

But What About Personal Fulfillment?

s I asked in the preface of this book, *how is it that* motherhood has taken such a nosedive in honor and respect in the last 20 years? Television doesn't seem to know how to portray moms. Teachers often encourage young girls not to "waste" their lives just being mothers. And women are continually encouraged to assert their intelligence and influence everywhere but in the home.

Many women, beginning with my generation, have acted as if motherhood were a brand of mediocrity to bear—if you can't make it in "the real world," at least you can always fall back on being a mother, but you'll have to live with the stigma. Yet now we see them on the evening news programs, their biological clocks running down, as they start to sense that maybe they *have* missed out and they go to unbelievable lengths to become what they've always shown disregard for—mothers.

Several times each year, my husband, Stu, and I travel to speak at weekend family conferences. During a break in my lecture one evening, a woman approached who had been reading ahead in the outline provided. She didn't like what she saw coming, and she told me there were things she wanted me to omit—things like the importance of mothering, how to raise kids, and making the family a priority.

She didn't want to hear anything about staying at home. She didn't want to hear anything about having kids. And she didn't want anyone making her feel guilty. She was a professor at a local university, and she wanted to stay in the classroom where she deserved to be.

I tried to explain graciously that what I would be presenting was generally applicable (after all, having kids is the only way to ensure future generations) and that I wouldn't have time to address all the exceptions. Since I was the speaker and already had my message prepared, and since I happen to believe what I was going to say and intended to say so anyway, she walked away in a huff.

After the break, as I stood to continue my talk, I saw her standing by the back door. She never left, but she never returned to her seat, either. I guess she was stationed near an escape route in case the pressure became too much. How sad to have made a decision and yet to feel so greatly intimidated by it.

She'll probably never change her mind. Maybe that's best. Maybe not. You may feel much the same. Or you may be confused, not knowing which route to take.

Let me offer an example of a friend who changed her mind about mothering. My two older sons both had her as a single teacher in high school. When they knew her, she was adamant about never having children. She once told her class, "If a baby fell out of the sky and landed in my lap, I wouldn't have an inkling of what to do with it."

Not long ago, I saw her at a ball game. She laughed as she told me, "You'll have to tell the boys to drop by the house when they're home from college. It's been an amazing transformation. They'll have to see it to believe it."

What would they have to see to believe? She's not only happily married, but she's now the mother of a baby boy as well. And the transformation *has* been amazing. She even wrote to me after learning I was writing this book:

> "I don't ever want to have kids!"
>
> I wonder how many times in my life I've said those words? Hundreds probably. And I really meant it. If there was ever anyone who was sure about not having children, it was me!
>
> Now here I sit, a 37-year-old mother of a 6-

month-old baby, and I laugh as those words echo in my memory! Describing what my son means to me is an impossible task. I could never put down in words the feelings I have when I'm doing all those things mothers do, feeding him, changing him, comforting him, playing with him, holding him, or watching him sleep.

The joy I get from taking care of this helpless little human being and knowing that I'm there for him when he needs me is immeasurable! He's such a precious little one. I can't imagine my life without him. He's added a different dimension to who I am. He's helped me to focus on someone other than myself, in the process making me a more caring person, I think, toward everyone else in my life.

I still work. I love my job teaching high-school English, and I always will. But I've cut back my schedule, and now I only teach part-time. Instead of being the sole fulfillment in my life, as it was for so many years, now it's only a part of my life. Real living begins when I pick up my baby after school and head home to be a mom. I'm a changed person, and I love it!

All the people in my life who heard me for so many years say I didn't want kids would be proud of me. Being a mother is the best choice I ever made. Motherhood is terrific!

Elisabeth Elliot quotes a mother, Brenda Sawyer, who says, "I can't think of another career more challenging and satisfying than to pour my energies into the daily task of making order out of chaos, music out of noise, communication out of babble, purposefulness out of purposelessness, pointing chubby little wayward feet gently toward the Path, lighting ignorance with knowledge and confusion with understanding."[1]

Another good example is Dr. Mary Ann Froehlich. She holds a "doctorate in music education/music therapy from the University of Southern California, an MA degree in Theology (pastoral care) from Fuller Theological Seminary, and MA and BM degrees in piano and harp performance and music therapy.

"She is also a certified Child Life Specialist and has published her dissertation research on the use of music therapy with chronically and terminally ill children.

"A Suzuki music educator and Registered Music Therapist—Board Certified, Mary Ann has worked in hospitals, schools, churches, and private practice. She is a frequent contributor to professional journals. Her piano/harp arrangements [have been published as well]." [2]

And her attitude toward mothering?

> When I was working and in graduate school, more than one person asked me why I was working so hard. Wasn't it all going to be wasted when I stopped to have a family? Why didn't I stop to have children now and "get it over with," and pursue my career later? They made motherhood sound like a prison term, a bad pill to swallow, a time for putting life on hold. Raising a family was posed as the antithesis of growing, learning, thinking, and contributing a specialization.
>
> I have found family life to be quite the opposite. Not only is this the most enjoyable time of my life, but also my children are the most stimulating and challenging teachers I've had yet, and they have tapped every resource in my background. [3]

Those women use strong words describing their experience as mothers: "immeasurable, precious, a new dimension, real living, terrific, nothing more challenging and satisfying, the most enjoyable time of my life, stimulating." Does that sound

I challenge you to make a
list of women you know,
one column for those who
have become mothers,
another for those who have
discounted motherhood and
focused their attention
elsewhere. Which ones
seem truly happier?

like a stigma to bear? Does that sound like wasted, unfulfilled living?

Don't listen only to the call of the politically correct, who tell you not to stay home and bake cookies but to get out there and make something of yourself. Sure you have rights to be your own person. But your children have rights, too. Among them is the right to be properly nurtured and given a strong foundation upon which to build their lives.

Look behind those messages. Look at the lives of the messengers. I challenge you to make a list of women you know, one column for those who have become mothers, another for those who have discounted motherhood and focused their attention elsewhere. Which ones seem truly happier? Which ones are more content, more at peace with themselves? Which ones have really been laying up more treasures for their later years? And if you had to live out the last few years of either kind of life, which would you choose?

Yes, some women cannot become mothers. Others have lost their children. Some simply have not felt adequate or gifted for the task and have avoided it. I have no criticism to aim at them.

I do take exception to those, though, who bad-mouth and denounce motherhood. How arrogant! Do they think they were produced by a color copier and a FAX machine? Are they really unaware that many of the personal strengths they now flaunt, they owe to their mothers, either through inherited genes or acquired skills at the feet of or thanks to the efforts of their mothers?

Motherhood is not an entry-level service position for mindless, insecure, second-class citizens. It is the noblest of callings. To be entrusted with the very life, health, and well-being of a tiny human person is a great gift and honor. To realize this small child reflects traits and characteristics of you, your spouse, and your families is a mind-shattering and heart-rending realization. To invest your time and best efforts into a child and to watch him grow, develop, and excel is to be part of the creative majesty of life itself.

Never let anyone denounce motherhood or dissuade you from experiencing it. As the three ladies in this chapter have told you, it transcends all other experiences.

> No other success in life—not being President, or
> being wealthy, or going to college, or writing a
> book, or anything else—comes up to the success of
> the man or woman who can feel that they have
> done their duty and that their children and grand-
> children rise up and call them blessed.

>   —Theodore Roosevelt, 1917

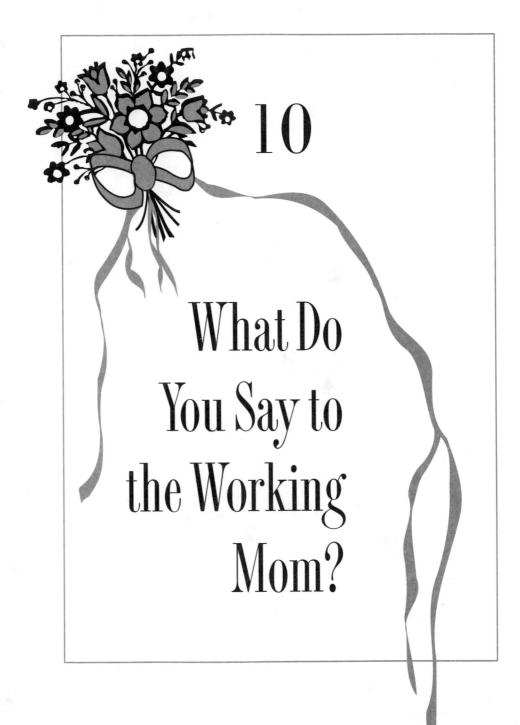

10

What Do You Say to the Working Mom?

*f I'm convinced of anything, it's that there is one* nonnegotiable in the discussion of working moms—the welfare of our children. If we're sacrificing that, we're making a terrible mistake. We must do all we can to develop the hearts and spirits of our children. Beyond that, though, there are probably fewer black and white answers than we might like.

I've expressed repeatedly my strong belief that I needed to be home with my three active boys when they were little. I was convinced then that I was doing the right thing, and I believe it still. But much—very much—has to do with the circumstances, the season of life, and the personalities within your family. What may be best in one home might be quite different in another.

In our situation, I have been, at one point, a stay-at-home mother, and I feel it was the best thing I could have done. I strongly recommend it when your children are young. I think it is very important for their development. At another season, I've been a part-time working mother, I've totally enjoyed it, and I had a clear conscience that it did not harm my boys. But even then, I couldn't simply change my focus away from mothering, assuming the kids were old enough that it wouldn't affect them.

If you're considering a job outside the home, I would encourage you, *work in addition to mothering, never in lieu of mothering.*

Children have different needs at different ages. Mothers have different levels of talent, strength, and capacity to meet those needs. Husbands have different levels of expertise, understanding, and availability to help Mom with all her responsibilities. Every family is unique, and even within each family, needs change with different seasons of life. *So we should be less concerned about having the right answers and more concerned about meeting the right needs.*

My friend Sharon sets the stage well to begin this discussion:

> I think we often fight the wrong battle—alienating those mothers who work from those who don't. These are two groups who should be in the trenches together. Rather than discussing the issue of working or not working outside the home, we need to address the issue of nurturing those in our homes—both our husbands and our children. When we address that issue, all the incidentals will fall into place. Women are going to work outside the home—any reading of current literature reflects that. Rather than keep fighting each other, we need to face the true enemy. We need to remember that the real battle is for our children.
>
> Stay-at-home mothers don't like to be stereotyped as sitting on their backsides, eating bon bons, watching soap operas. And working moms don't like to be stereotyped as walking out the door with briefcase in hand, ignoring their children, ready to pay any price to advance their careers.
>
> "Career women" and "working women" are not synonymous—and yet many times that's how it's portrayed. Mothers can work outside the home without being preoccupied with their careers to the detriment of their families.
>
> At the same time, "stay-at-home moms" and "nurturing moms" are not synonymous, either—yet that's how they're often portrayed as well. I have friends who looked forward to the day their children

were born and now look forward to the day they're gone. The only time they seem to enjoy them in the interim is when they perform to their liking. Being a stay-at-home mom doesn't mean you'll automatically be a nurturing mom.

The truth is, stereotypes just don't work. And being at home is not the goal. Making the biggest impact in your home is the goal. Though proximity is critically important, we cannot assume that our proximity alone will automatically ensure success. Being around and being attentive are both needed. Some mothers stay at home and yet have, to a degree, emotionally abandoned their children.

What's more, as my counselor friend Denny reminds us, there are no guarantees, even if you do all the right things. Many good parents have experienced great disappointment with children who seemed to have had the right environment and yet made all the wrong decisions.

The real objective is to work hard to determine all those right things you must do as a parent and to make good decisions based on a realistic evaluation of your family's needs.

What concerns should we have about working moms? In a poll of 30,000 women, *Parents* magazine asked if a woman can have it all—both a career and motherhood—and only 54 percent said yes.[1] Reservations obviously exist.

I would agree as well. A woman can have it all—just not all at once. I believe a woman can have a successful career. I believe a woman can be a very good mother. I even believe a woman can work outside the home and be a good mother. What I truly doubt is whether a woman can pursue a full-time career and be an effective mother at the same time. A full-strength effort can only go so far, as many women recognize.

You may criticize her choice, but at least give Paula Zahn, co-host of "CBS This Morning," credit for honesty when she said, "I must settle for being less of a mom today to be a better worker. You can't be great at everything at one time. Something's got to give."[2]

Paula, for reasons known only to herself, chose to be a better worker/career woman and a lesser mother. It would seem she placed her or her employer's needs over her child's. "I had a very loving mother who was always there," she continued, "and I want to be the same, but I can't. I'm a different kind of mom with a different set of demands."[3]

Working and pursuing a career are very different in my mind. Sometimes work is necessary, as it was for my mom. In Sharon's case, who quickly draws the distinction between career mother and working mother, she also felt she had little choice about working.

> One of the reasons I went back to work was that it was either Dennis adding another job or me picking up part-time work. It wasn't because we were trying to move up the financial ladder—we were just in a critical stage. We felt very strongly that the added hours of a second job for Dennis would be detrimental to his relationship with his children. We even discussed this with the kids at the time, and they wanted me to work part-time—they didn't want to give up more time with their dad.

Now she works a part-time, flexible schedule, more to make a positive impact in her community than for the sake of family finances. She's just geared to run the race at a fast pace. The challenge and the accomplishments of her job bring her great satisfaction.

But there is a danger we need to be alert to—getting the

working ahead of the nurturing. In her book *Can Motherhood Survive?* Connie Marshner writes, "All of Western civilization is now being enveloped by a miasma of anti-motherhood, and few of us can escape its effects. . . . I made some very serious mistakes when I was a career-centered mother, and I know that plenty of other mothers, even well-intentioned Christian mothers, are repeating the very same mistakes today."[4]

There's the warning flag again—she was a "career-centered mother" making "serious mistakes" in raising her kids. We should heed her warning.

My son Kent wrote to me of a woman in one of his psychology classes who cried as she told the class of her career mind-set when her kids were little. They never enjoyed extracurricular activities after school because there was no one there to shuttle them back and forth. They missed out on those experiences, and they still feel the loss. She regrets her choices and has had to deal with the consequences. Even today, she isn't included in her kids' lives the way she'd like to be. Yesterday, she was too busy for them. Today, following in her footsteps, they've become too busy for her. They aren't responding to the fact that she worked but to the fact that, in their minds, her work became more important than they were.

Helen Hayes, the first lady of the American theater, enjoyed a great deal of success as an actress. But later in life, she admitted she wished she had spent more time with her family. "For all the deep satisfaction it gave me," she said, "my career was not a good thing for us (her husband and herself) or for the children."[5]

Let's keep in mind that a successful balancing of work and motherhood requires more than just planning your day carefully. Focus on the Family founder Dr. James Dobson writes:

> There's only so much energy within the human
> body for expenditure each 24 hours. And when it is
> invested in one place it is not available for use in

another. Few women alive today are equipped with the super strength necessary at the end of a work-day to meet all the emotional needs of their children. To train and guide and discipline. To build self-esteem in them. To teach the true values of life, and beyond that, to maintain a healthy marital relationship as well. To the contrary, I have observed that exhausted wives and mothers become irritable, grouchy, and frustrated, setting the stage for conflict within the home.[6]

What a tragedy to rationalize or buy into the message that you can do it all and that you deserve it, and then to find you've come up short at the expense of those you love most. Let's make sure we're finding a balance—not a compromise where both sides lose, but a balance where we can do one thing well without taking away from the more important thing that *must* be done well.

Years ago, we invited several church leaders and their wives to our house for a formal dinner. I had worked hard all week to prepare a gourmet meal. I had rehearsed each step, every recipe. This was going to be a pleasurable experience, an evening they would not forget. Well, unfortunately, that's how it worked out. I'm sure they'll never forget that fiasco.

I wanted to be a good hostess as my guests arrived, and I purposely took time to enjoy conversation with each of them. After appetizers and some small talk, everyone stepped to the table to find his or her place.

As I prepared to serve our guests, I realized the soup I had made had burned. All my special ingredients were lost. I actually had to throw it out. I hadn't been there stirring it as the recipe instructed.

Earlier that day, I'd driven 50 miles round-trip to buy very special dinner rolls from a certain restaurant. I opened my oven door to find that they, too, had burned while I had been

Let's make sure we're finding a balance—not a compromise where both sides lose, but a balance where we can do one thing well without taking away from the more important thing that *must* be done well.

preoccupied with my guests.

Even the main course of my gourmet dinner was a disaster. I hadn't timed it right.

I had planned well. I had purchased all the right ingredients. I had done my best. I simply wasn't able to do all the things called for that night. I couldn't be in two places at once.

The experience taught me I can't be in two places at once in life, either. And my caution to you is simple: Don't push too hard. Don't try to take on too much. You might see others who seem to pack 48 hours into 24. They don't. Yes, some are much faster than others. Some of you can accomplish a great deal. But don't assume you can be in two places at once. Don't think you can pack 48 hours into 24. It's a lie.

My one-quart saucepan holds just one quart no matter how much I pour into it. Something is being lost over the edge if I try to pour in more. People can't keep cramming more into their lives, either. Something is being ignored, omitted, or lost.

Know your capacity. Keep your priorities well in mind. Then go ahead and work if it will be rewarding to you. Just don't work at the expense of your children.

One last caution. Some may assume that if you can't be in two places at once, simply do two things in one place—do paying work in the home, as I suggested in chapter 8. Here, too, approach it wisely, and don't make groundless assumptions.

Being a pastor's wife, it was inevitable that individuals would seek me out for advice and counsel. When the church was small and our older boys were young—probably two and four—I did a great deal of counseling over the phone. It seemed the perfect thing to do; I could help people and still be at home.

But with people expressing their deepest fears and concerns, you have to keep your full attention riveted on them. You can't have noise surrounding you. You can't be interrupted with childish questions and requests. You need to be left alone to concentrate. And you never know when a call is going to come or how long it will last.

This ministry of mine frustrated the boys more than I realized. One day, one of them got my attention.

We had an old upright piano that was a prized family possession. One of the wooden knobs on the keyboard cover had a screw that had been stripped. It would sit in place for appearance' sake, but if you pulled on it, it would come right out. On that fateful day, one of my boys, weary of being shushed and shooed again, took his frustrations out on my prize. He pulled the wooden knob from its cradle and used the exposed screw to scribble all over the wooden front. I got the message.

Those scars in the finish remain to this day. They remind me of my careless attention to their needs. I thought my proximity ensured my success. I didn't give much attention to the season of the boys' lives and their particular needs. For me, the consequences were only scars on my piano. I saw my mistake and changed. Thank heaven those were the only scars caused by my inattention.

What do I say to a working mother? Don't feel guilty if you have to work, even if you just *want* to work, as long as your work is a balance, not a compromise; thought through, not a rationalization. Reconsider if you think you can pursue a full-time career and be a truly successful mother at the same time. You can probably have it all. Just don't try to have it all at once. Your children will be with you so few years. Focus on them and make work secondary. After they're gone, you'll have plenty of time to pursue a career.

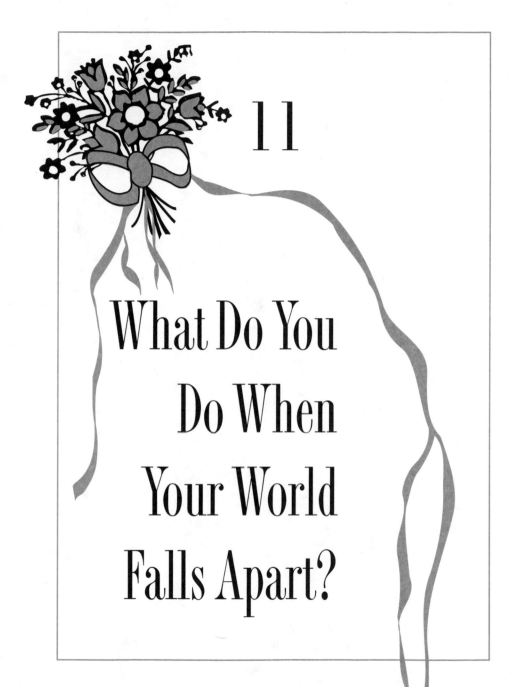

11

What Do You Do When Your World Falls Apart?

*ometimes life is hard. Sometimes being a mother is* hard, too—maybe even overwhelming. You may have had crises and disasters come so unexpectedly, and they may have so devastated you, that you ask, "What about me? What am I to do? I can't take your advice. It's too late. What you warned of has already happened—all of it and much more." Or you may say, "You didn't say anything about those catastrophes we have no influence over—medical problems, handicaps, deaths. How in the world am I to face such problems when I have no power to influence or correct them?"

In short, you may feel as if your world has fallen apart and there's nothing you can do to put it back together. Perhaps not because of past events but present circumstances, you feel life will never be normal again, and you're having trouble holding on.

I've thought a lot about the issues many of my friends face every day. Overwhelming, paralyzing issues. I couldn't begin to address them all. And if I tried, I wouldn't do them justice. But as I've turned those problems over in my mind—categorizing them, weighing them, looking for encouragement—several approaches have come to mind that I think bear consideration.

Finding solutions is never simple, and when you do find them, working them out is seldom easy. But regardless of what you face, Mom, I believe the ten suggestions that follow can give you hope and bring you strength. Don't discount them quickly. Don't brush them off because an illustration doesn't match your circumstances. Pain paralyzes, and you're too special to be held captive under the weight of pain you may be bearing. So look for the application to your circumstance. Imagine how you could use each suggestion actively to your advantage.

1. Never give up.

"Never give up" is the first advice I give single mothers. As long as you're trying, you're winning. Only when you give up do you lose.

That doesn't mean you have to overcome every obstacle. It doesn't mean you have to win the battle today or tomorrow or even this year. It just means you will always commit yourself to taking one more step.

It doesn't mean you never take a break, either. Taking a break from your circumstance or your surroundings is not only a temporary relief, but it can help you gain perspective as well.

Instead, it means never saying, "I can't handle this anymore, and I won't try." How can you know how close you might be to that breakthrough? How can you know how near you are to finally seeing things in a new light that will give you the strength and determination to deal with the situation? How can you know how close help may be?

If you think you can, you probably can—no matter what the issue at hand. If you think you can't, you probably can't. Never giving up is saying, "I think I can." No matter how small you feel your chances are of succeeding, you know you have no chance if you give up. So beware.

If you find your strength waning as you compare yourself with "successful" moms around you, remember that comparisons are deadly. Those moms are real people, too. Every one has her own problems and obstacles to overcome. You just don't see the deep water she may have come through. Successful people aren't those who have never faced dilemmas. They're the ones who never gave up despite the dilemmas. And that can be you, too.

2. Grieve your loss.

You may have experienced great loss in a number of ways. You may not even fully realize all the losses you've faced. Loss can be material, relational, or perceptional. The way your physical body functions may have been significantly altered. Your role in life may have changed dramatically.

When loss does occur, a process called *grief* needs to happen for recovery to take place. And that may require some outside assistance.

Please don't confuse pressing on through pain with pushing it away—out of sight, out of mind, out of reach. We have to deal with it, to go through a process of coming to terms with the situation and growing beyond it. But that's too much of a process to adequately develop within the confines of this book.

Basically, you must face what has happened and identify the loss. You must acknowledge your feelings and admit to and submit to the pain you've tried to deny or hold back. The process will enable you to discover new insights into what has taken place and how to apply those insights in beginning to move on.

Progressing from what was to what is requires unlearning old patterns and learning new ones—new ways of life, new states of mind. It also takes perseverance and time, but with liberal doses of both, you will grow.

I have two dear friends who both suffered the loss of their husbands and sons within a short period. As a result, they've learned a lot about this process firsthand. One of them, Jackie, now helps others work through their grief. She always encourages them to allow themselves to go through the process rather than deny it, to let their hearts feel and process the pain. Stuffing your feelings doesn't make them go away. It just shoves them below the surface, where they can fester unattended.

Grieving your loss will help you gain perspective and show you how to heal. It will help you accept responsibility for moving on. And it will help you release your anger and forgive instead of thrusting your anger on undeserving family and friends.

And never grieve alone. Search out a friend who will help you, someone you can trust. Work through it, and don't deny it. You'll be better off.

3. Get help.

Whether for lack of direction, pride, or confusion, we're often slow to get help. But we're frequently in desperate need of another perspective, special insight, or specific training to help us through crises.

Mom, maybe you're in deep pain, and you just need a trusted friend who will listen, who will be there, and who will walk with you through the pain. Isolation will only hinder your recovery. If a friend can't help, look for a support group where you can find encouragement and understanding.

Maybe you have needs that require special resources—it could be relief help with a handicapped child. It could be equipment to deal with a medical condition.

Maybe you have concerns that are paralyzing you or past hurts that plague you that need to be explored. Perhaps you need a professional to guide you. There's no way you can be capable of meeting all your own needs or sorting out all your own problems. And don't allow anyone to make you feel there is some stigma to seeking wise counsel. Avoiding counsel may only prevent you from enjoying a more fulfilled life.

Maybe your crisis requires the kind of help that will cost money, but you're reluctant to commit yourself. If you need help, however, do what you must to find it. Financial assistance is often available. The bottom line: Smart people get help.

4. Cherish your relationships.

Problems have a way of isolating us from others. Just when we most need those we care about, we often feel least willing to be with them. What a paradox!

Don't cut yourself off. Don't destroy relationships through neglect or rejection. Isolation can be one of the most devastating aspects of any crisis. Don't cut off lifelines in your time of greatest need. If anything, give extra nourishment to those relationships. Take time to reflect on their importance and cherish them.

In a commencement address to the graduates of Wellesley College in 1990, then-First-Lady Barbara Bush encouraged her listeners to make a different kind of investment—an investment in relationships. "At the end of your life," she told them, "you will never regret not having passed one more test, not winning one more verdict or closing one more deal. You will regret time not spent with a husband, a friend, a child or a parent."[1]

5. Admit your failures—and then move on.

We can cause ourselves a great deal of insecurity and distress by trying to avoid looking at ourselves realistically, refusing to admit any blame or failure. Avoiding failure won't make it go away; it will just make it loom larger.

We all make mistakes, but too many of us refuse to admit them. It's too threatening to look in the mirror and see our errors. It seems easier to deny them and move on. But nothing changes when we deny making mistakes. We don't learn. We don't adjust. We don't correct our course.

None of us can foresee the future. Few of us can see the present all that clearly. Often that's why we find ourselves not knowing what hit us. But when the dilemma has our attention, that's the best time to look at it realistically, to see what went wrong, and to learn how to avoid having it happen again.

All of us need to analyze our particular circumstances. After we've considered where we might have failed, we need to learn from it, chalk it up to experience, set it aside, and move on.

6. Keep loving.

Sometimes we're not the ones who bring on the crisis but the victims. Maybe your children have caused you pain by their actions, their choices, or their life-styles.

Don't confuse your rejection of those poor choices with your rejection of those you love. Disapprove foolish choices, but don't reject the child who made them. The loss you incur by doing that will only add to your pain. It won't help it. It won't justify it. It won't heal it. It will only intensify it.

Love is the one commodity we always have enough of. It's the only thing in life that is not diminished by being divided and shared. It's the only thing we have the freedom to give away lavishly. No matter how much love we give, we'll never run out. We'll never find there's too little left to share.

And most of all, love is the most certain healer—of you, of the situation, of the others involved. Make sure it's spontaneous. Make sure it's unconditional—especially when it's least deserved. That's what makes love different. Real love is often given despite the circumstances. It's acceptance when someone isn't acceptable. And that's when we all need it most. I think you'll find plenty of situations where that applies, don't you?

7. Don't dominate.

It's easy, in crises, to either be overwhelmed and paralyzed or to try to take control. Sometimes taking control of a situation is exactly what you should do—if you're supposed to be the one in charge. But it's not good if you're trying to "fix" the people involved. A domineering mother tends to do that, to try to manipulate people into acting the way she thinks is best.

A domineering mother can be one of the most dangerous and damaging parts of any crisis. That negative influence probably accounts for as many disorders as any other factor in the lives of children. Unfortunately, many such mothers don't have a clue that they are part of a problem.

One study states, "In homes led by dominant mothers, both girls and boys were likely to say that they disliked the opposite sex. Also, these girls and boys were frequently disliked by the opposite sex."[2] Many experts believe maternal dominance has a

Love is the one
commodity we
always have
enough of.
It's the only thing
in life that is not
diminished by being
divided and shared.

direct and extremely influential link to sexual disorientation: "Boys from homes in which the mother asserted herself as the leader exhibited more feminine sex-role preferences than did boys from homes in which the father was the leader."[3]

I've seen a number of homes where Mom had wanted her child to be a certain sex. When she didn't get what she wanted, she directed that child's life, possibly unconsciously, into the realm of being the little girl or little boy she preferred. The consequences were devastating.

8. Be creative.

When we're stuck in bad situations and seem powerless to break free, it's because we continue to see the situation in the same light and see the same obstacles as overwhelming. When we bring creativity to a situation, we can begin to see it from a different angle, and we can think of new solutions or ways of handling the problems day to day.

Mom, it may be little more than your monotonous schedule that has you frustrated. Don't allow yourself to get bogged down because you don't have the energy to change. Don't let lack of funds, painful experiences, or other handicaps cause you to live under a low-hanging black cloud.

Move, Mom, move! Creativity never blossomed in the midst of comfort and ease. It's stimulated by need. If you have need, channel that energy into finding solutions. Think about it. You're more creative than you realize. You just have to apply yourself. It takes the right attitude, and it takes action. Once you get started, you might be surprised where it will take you.

Creativity often opens the door to changes that can amaze and refresh us. There's always a way to lighten the load. And once again, don't be afraid to ask for help.

9. Let the process refine you.

Heat both melts butter and hardens steel. The effect depends on what a substance is made of. Fire can either destroy or purify.

Shaun is severely afflicted with cerebral palsy. When he was born, his parents, Terry and Cheryl, were faced with myriad decisions. Probably the least obvious at the time, but the most critical over the long haul, was the decision of whether they would allow Shaun's condition to destroy them or refine them. Statistics indicate that most people don't make a conscious decision on that issue, and the weight of their trials destroys them. More than 80 percent of all marriages involving a handicapped child end in divorce.

But Terry and Cheryl made a lot of good decisions. And the most important was that choice not to let Shaun's condition ruin them or their marriage. From the moment of his birth, they knew what they had to do. As Terry said, "He's our son, and we'll love him no matter what."

Life hasn't been easy since they made that decision. Loving hasn't been easy, either. They've learned that love is giving yourself unselfishly to another. Through the years of interrupted sleep, constant care, and the never ending routine of accomplishing even the most basic tasks, they've matured. There hasn't been much room for selfishness or self-pity. There has been too much to do. But instead of their sacrifice making them less, it has made them more—more loving, more compassionate, more faithful. It has built their character and refined their marriage. Cheryl confided to me,

> Sometimes, we're so tired, we feel we can't go on. But God has always given us everything we need and never more than we can handle.
>
> Our son has helped us become tough, and at the same time, tender. He sees life differently than I do. Time has little meaning to him. Each day is new. A friend's touch, the smell of a flower, a new taste, a funny song—they all bring delight to his day. When I take the time to see life through his eyes, it's sweet and wonderful. God is very near to me then.

Shaun can't speak, so I watch his eyes and his hands as they express his mood, his desires, and his feelings. I have to slow down to understand him. Sometimes, his expressions are so quiet, I have to listen with my heart and try to feel what he feels. When I do, I think I see life a little clearer.

In Shaun's world, it's as if all the distractions have been taken away. What's left is what's truly real.

This experience has been the most difficult trial and yet the deepest pleasure of my life, and perhaps with it I've been given a glimpse into the heart of God.

Their process has obviously refined them. I hope it encourages you to allow your ordeal to refine you as well.

10. Stop looking back and wishing.

Whatever the problem, whatever the crisis, it's natural to look back to the way things used to be, to wish things hadn't changed. A little of that is to be expected. But too much of it keeps us from moving on to change our circumstances for the better.

Dwelling on the "what if's" does nothing to help us. Instead, it leaves us paralyzed. You may have done nothing at all to deserve the problems you face. As I've told my boys so many times, life isn't always fair, and unfortunately, we have to get used to that.

For all the mental powers we're supposed to have, when it comes to living life, we pretty much have one-track minds. We can focus on the future, or we can keep rerunning tapes of the past. You can't change yesterday, Mom. But you can determine what you'll do tomorrow. It isn't easy, but it's possible. You may not have made the bad things happen to you, but today, you can begin making good things happen. Just stop looking back and wishing it had been different. Instead, look forward and begin planning how to make your desires for yourself and your family come true. *You can do it.*

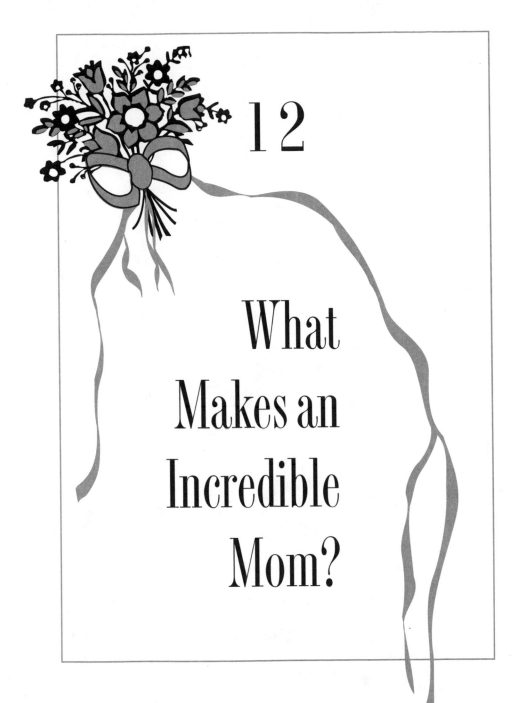

12

What
Makes an
Incredible
Mom?

here's a wall in our home that has become precious to us. It will never be painted. It will never be scrubbed. And when we move from that house, I'll probably find a way to take the plasterboard along and frame it.

The boys always backed up to that wall over the years to be measured and see how they were growing. The wall was their standard. It was their measuring stick to determine how much progress they'd made since the last measurement. They were anxious to know, "How am I doing? How do I measure up?"

Do you ever wonder how you're doing, how effective your mothering is?

One day Stu and I were sitting in a little restaurant in Chicago. "I'll bet that lady is a great mom," Stu said of our waitress. Here was a server who was in touch with her customers. She didn't just go through the motions, she was engaging. She really looked at people, and she talked *to* them, not *at* them. She really listened and interacted. She had a bright, winning way that was contagious. And she made people feel important. What a profile for an incredible mom! She just looked as though she measured up. We even told her we had her pegged as being a good mom and having some very lucky kids.

Do you wish there were a wall you could back up to so you could see how much you've grown, how you compare with the standards you've set? If I could make a measuring wall for you, I would pencil in some of the standards that make up the rest of this chapter. "Grow toward these," I'd encourage.

1. Am I creating a *positive* environment?

Is it so inviting at your house that the kids take shortcuts to bring their friends home? Is there a positive attitude in the air? Do they see you as a friend, one interested in their day, their activities, and their needs, or do they see you more as the resident grouch?

If we want our kids to express happy hearts, it has to begin with us. It has to be caught before it can be taught. And if we can instill positive attitudes in them, positive actions will result.

It has become a natural part of our culture to be sarcastic, to put things down, to be a complainer. But when we fall into that habit, it affects our whole attitude, and soon we feel that things are bad and unfair and that we deserve better. People with absolutely wonderful lives can become frustrated and depressed just because the trend of negative attitudes has taken hold of them.

What kind of atmosphere are you creating in your home? Are you capitalizing on the joys of family life and minimizing the hard things? There may be a lot you could get discouraged about, but what good would that do you? It may not be natural for you, but stop and begin to count your blessings. Focus on the good. And when your kids do the same thing, reinforce it.

At our house, I often thank the boys for saying thank you. That's positive reinforcement, and it has lasting effects.

Finding nice things to say needs to be a forever rule. At dinner, especially, make it a time to enjoy one another, not to gripe and complain. Just like praise and criticism, you need ten positive statements to balance out every negative statement.

When the boys tended to start complaining, I would sing a little song, "Oh, be thankful for the good things that you've got."[1] The end of that verse continued to instruct them and remind them of why and what their response should be. The boys have heard that from me more than enough. Now when they catch themselves complaining, they anticipate my response and say, "Don't say it. I know, be thankful for the good things that you've got."

That's right. They got it, and it is working.

Mom, I encourage you to give attention to spotting the traps of negative thinking in your house and steer your children away from them. As a result, your family will more likely enjoy:

- thankfulness instead of grumbling
- confidence rather than doubts
- peace rather than conflicts
- trust rather than suspicion
- certainty instead of apprehension
- rest instead of restlessness
- security instead of fear
- freedom rather than bondage

and much more.

2. Am I creating an environment that's *motivational?*

In a letter from college, Blake was expressing his appreciation for the motivation he received at home. It worked for him, and he sees it working in others as well.

> As I've had the chance to work with a few specific freshmen on the floor this year, I've seen that the key is showing love and letting them see that you care about them and trust them as important individuals. That's enough to turn the most introverted or arrogant around into a smiling guy who wants to be around you.

It works at home, too, as you love them and let them see how much you care. Sacrificing your time, energy, and talent for them speaks loudly. Kids usually grow up to be like their parents, whether they want to or not, because they live out what they've seen modeled. What are you modeling for your kids? Are you that quiet, steady, supportive influence that calms the storms and makes them feel important?

3. Am I creating an environment where we really *communicate?*

Communication is more than just being there when they want to talk. Listening is crucial, and your kids need to know you'll listen—really listen—when they have hard things they need to discuss.

But with teenagers, you're probably going to have to stimulate the conversation. It's in those unplanned, informal times that they're most likely to open up on the difficult subjects. You have to be stimulating those times, however. After all, if both of you aren't comfortable talking casually, where will they find the setting to bring up that hard-to-discuss topic? You have to have a track record with them to make them feel secure in expressing their fears, doubts, and disappointments.

In the process of all this communicating, you're able to have a finger on the pulse of your family. You're able to know where each is headed and when one might be drifting off course.

By knowing where the hurts lie and the concerns rest, you'll know why a need must be met *now.* You'll be alerted to step in and take action in the most appropriate way.

Leave notes, if necessary, to communicate plans for the day, expectations, appointments. Children just naturally develop their own daily agendas if you don't remind them of duties or expectations. You can eliminate a lot of "Oh, Mom" if you communicate so your kids can plan your schedule into theirs.

4. Am I creating an environment that's *safe?*

We're usually pretty good about explaining boundaries when our kids are little: Stay away from the street. Don't touch the stove burner—it might be hot. Don't speak to strangers.

But as the kids grow older, we sometimes assume they'll know things by osmosis. The result is that they cross lines they didn't realize existed. Then it's confusing to understand why they deserve discipline or other unpleasant consequences for their actions. Growing up becomes confusing at times like that.

Make sure you allow
yourself breaks—
a few breaths of
fresh air, a diversion
from time to time,
maybe a change
of scenery.

Drawing obvious lines and explaining expectations—stating the obvious from your perspective, if you will—gives your kids clear lane lines, boundaries, that also provide comfort zones. As long as they stay within the boundaries, they know they're okay with you. Their environment feels safe. And if they cross the lines, they understand why they're being disciplined or left to suffer the consequences for what they've done. Those lines might relate to homework, dating, household chores, language, curfews, and so on.

I try to put messages I want our boys to remember into jingles or sayings that hopefully embed themselves in their subconscious. One such reminder was of three things that cause teenagers trouble when they drive: food, friends, and music. Then one of the boys hopped in his car one day, cranked up the radio, and started backing out of the garage. He left a crease the entire length of his dad's pickup and crunched the right rear fender of his car before realizing what was happening.

"Couldn't you hear the metal scraping?" we asked.

"No, I had my music turned up," he responded.

"Didn't you feel some resistance as you accelerated?"

"Yeah, but I thought maybe it was a shrub or something."

But we don't have any shrubs growing in the middle of our driveway! The problem wasn't just that he couldn't hear the noise; he was so attuned to the music that he wasn't aware of what was happening around him.

He didn't recall my warnings that time. But he found out they were valid. He understood he had crossed a boundary. And he understood painfully why he would be suffering consequences as a result of his actions.

So set out the lane lines, Mom. Give them a fresh coat of paint every once in a while so your kids don't forget where they run. As you do, you'll be creating a safe environment for everyone.

5. What about me? Is my life *balanced?*

Are you taking care of yourself? After all, how can you care for others if you haven't taken care of yourself? What does the airline flight attendant tell you as you begin each flight? If there's an emergency and you're with a child, put on your own oxygen mask first. Then you'll have the stamina and presence of mind to assist your child. Life sort of works that way, too.

Make sure you allow yourself breaks—a few breaths of fresh air, a diversion from time to time, maybe a change of scenery.

Every mom should build into her schedule something to look forward to each day. It doesn't have to be a big thing. Maybe it's a promise to yourself to enjoy a long, hot bath. Maybe a half hour with a special book. Maybe a drive all alone.

If you have a physical or emotional problem, find help. Zero in on the causes, and find solutions. Your unattended wounds may be affecting more than just you. Their influence may be wounding family members as well. So don't feel guilty about taking care of yourself so you can really take care of those you love.

Accept yourself. Everyone has strengths and weaknesses. Learn to accept yourself in spite of your weaknesses. When you do, you'll probably find you're becoming more accepting of others as well—most importantly, your husband and kids. And what an essential step that is in being a good mom!

Give yourself away. It takes a great investment of yourself in the lives of your husband and children to be a truly incredible mom. Your involvement in your children's lives and activities (and expenses, which grow at the rate of the national debt) will speak volumes to your kids and leave an indelible imprint in their hearts.

Too many moms have given up that involvement and attention. As their focus has shifted, families have suffered, and so has society.

So live a balanced life. Make time for yourself. But don't be distracted. Approach motherhood with a passion.

6. Am I creating an environment that's *gracious*?

Has experience caused your family to expect kindness and understanding from you, or complaints and grumblings? Are you flexible or rigid?

If you've planned a family dinner and for various reasons no one shows up, do you make assumptions and attack the offenders, or can you withhold judgment and give each person room for presenting legitimate excuses?

Can you let your child and his friends build forts in your living room that stay there all day? That generosity may be remembered for a lifetime.

Do you have a "yes face"? Charles Swindoll tells a story reported by Dr. Karl Menninger about the importance of "yes faces":

> During his days as president, Thomas Jefferson and a group of companions were traveling across the country on horseback. They came to a river which had left its banks because of a recent downpour. The swollen river had washed the bridge away. Each rider was forced to ford the river on horseback, fighting for his life against the rapid currents. The very real possibility of death threatened each rider, which caused a traveler who was not part of their group to step aside and watch. After several had plunged in and made it to the other side, the stranger asked President Jefferson if he would ferry him across the river. The president agreed without hesitation. The man climbed on, and shortly thereafter the two of them made it safely to the other side. As the stranger slid off the back of the saddle onto dry ground, one in the group asked him, "Tell me, why did you select the president to ask this favor of?" The man was shocked, admitting he had no idea it was the president who had helped him.

"All I know," he said, "is that on some of your faces was written the answer 'No,' and on some of them was the answer 'yes.' His was a 'Yes' face."[2]

Do you have the kind of yes face that makes your kids feel comfortable asking? Does your yes face say, "It's okay to make mistakes; I'll still love you"? Do they feel as if you'll really listen to childish requests? Do they believe they're important enough that you'll react to their needs with flexibility?

Being gracious means making kids feel that "it's okay. Don't worry about it." Sometimes—more often than we think—kids need for someone to be gracious to them, especially when they don't deserve it. Come to think of it, don't we all? In fact, that's the whole meaning of grace—undeserved favor.

7. Am I being *diligent?*

Are you giving persistent, attentive care to your family?

A friend served cauliflower to her family one night when her son's friend was over. The boy had never seen cauliflower. At his house, his dad brings home a pizza or some other fast food almost every night. It's nice that his dad takes the time and spends the money to lighten his mom's load at dinnertime, but is that really the caring thing to do for the family? Is that the best choice or simply the easiest?

Well, how do you stand against the measuring wall? Is your profile looking good as you evaluate? Do you feel like a great mom?

Sometimes—no, frequently—you feel anything but great. The routine seems so predictable. The kids don't seem to notice your efforts. There's little time for yourself.

Don't give up, Mom. Don't feel as if you aren't measuring

up. You're doing the most important thing in the world. You're mothering. Some day the kids will recognize your efforts, your sacrifices, your support. Then they'll begin to show their appreciation. It almost always happens. Here's an example from an Ann Landers Mother's Day column:

Dear Mom:

I wish I could spend Mother's Day with you, but I can't, so I'm writing a letter and hope that you will read it in Ann Landers' column.

Mom, I love you so much. There are so many things that I didn't understand when I was young, but I understand them now.

I didn't have any idea how hard you worked and the burdens you carried until I traveled that road myself.

I didn't know how rough it was when you were having trouble with Dad and us kids, but I know now.

I didn't realize how lonely you were until I was lonely. I didn't realize how hurt you were until I was hurt the same way by my own children.

I didn't know how many times I could have made you happy by just saying, "I love you, Mom." But now I know, because those are the words I long to hear from my kids. Whoever said, "Life is the greatest teacher of all," knew what he was talking about.

When I was growing up, we had more than our share of battles. I remember how I thought you were too hard on me, because you insisted that I keep my room neat, turn off the TV and do my homework, hang up my clothes, do chores around the house and write thank-you notes right away.

You made me do a lot of things I didn't want to

do. You said it was good for my character. I couldn't see the connection. I thought you were nuts. But now I have kids of my own, I understand things a lot better. I am grateful that you didn't let me wear you down. Remembering your strength gives me strength to stand up to my own kids when they try to con me the way I tried to con you.

It seems like I found time for everything and everyone but you, Mom. It would have been easy to drop in for a cup of tea and a hug, but my friends came first. Would any of them have done for me what you did? I doubt it.

I remember the times you called on the phone, and I was in a hurry to get off. It makes me ashamed. I remember, too, the times I could have included you when my little family had outings, but I didn't.

It took me all my life to learn what a mother is. I guess it's impossible to know until you become a mother yourself. Believe me, now I know how rough you had it and how terrific you are.

Millions of people are going to read this column today, and they will see themselves. Some will feel uneasy, and that's okay, if they learn from it.

Time has a sneaky way of slipping away. We become so involved in getting from one day to the next that before we know it, the tomorrows are yesterdays. I hope this letter gives you an idea of how much I admire and respect you, Mom. You really are the greatest.[3]

You *are* the greatest, Mom! You understand value—not monetary value, but the kind that really counts. You understand the development of the heart and spirit. That's what has real lasting value. And that's where you need to invest the best of who you are—in the things that matter the most, so that the main thing will always remain the main thing.

It's true, Mom, you're incredible! You have every reason to feel good about who you are and what you do. God bless you!

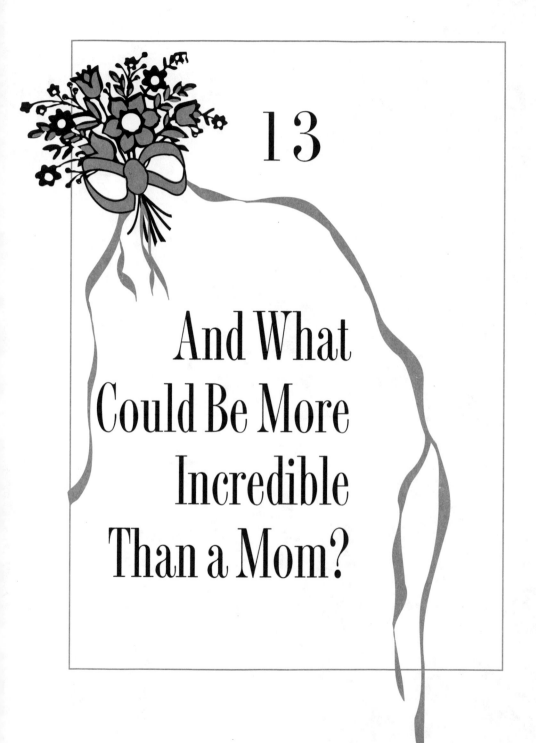

13

And What Could Be More Incredible Than a Mom?

*hat else but a mom and a dad, leading a family together.* Ever see a 1,000-piece puzzle assembled with only 500 pieces? Something's missing, like half the picture. Ever try to create a great dish from a recipe with missing or wrongly proportioned ingredients? It just doesn't come out right. Ask any new bride who didn't read the recipe carefully. Something's missing, and the final product tastes like it.

Our kids deserve the whole picture. They need all the parenting ingredients, namely a mom *and* a dad. The Master Designer wrote His parenting manual, the Bible, with the intention that each child should enjoy the influence of both a mother and a father. The completed puzzle shows the necessity of the masculine leader to ensure the growth of a strong family.

No book can address all the aspects of being a mother and a wife. In this book, I'm focusing on the incredible impact of mothering, and as a result, little has been said of fathers. But obviously, whatever impact is made by a mother can only be made stronger by the additional impact of a father. After all, the best strength is combined strength.

Consider this from an issue of *Our Daily Bread:*

> In a horse-pulling contest at a county fair, the first-place horse moved a sled weighing 4,500 pounds. The runner-up had pulled 4,000 pounds. The owners of the two horses wondered how much the animals could pull if they worked together. So they hitched them up and loaded the sled. To everyone's

surprise, the horses were able to pull 12,000 pounds.[1]

Combined strength, synergism—doing more together than they could individually. And more than that, they displayed strength combining the best of both individuals, filling in the shortcomings of each. In the movie *Rocky*, the hero comments on the relationship between himself and his very different girl-friend, Adrian: "I got gaps. She's got gaps. Together, we got no gaps."

What Rocky had discovered, for all his perceived ignorance, was really quite insightful. He had noted an abiding principle. He and Adrian were different. Even more basically, men and women are different. Yes, different. Equal, yes; same, no. And in that principle rests a key to balanced, successful parenting. When we learn, as men and women, to accept and even cele-brate our differences, our marriages and homes will take on an atmosphere we have all dreamed of from the beginning. And, happily, our children will be more likely to grow up to become confident, secure, effective adults.

We're often tempted to look at our differences with our mates as frustrations instead of realizing the strength that can come from our diversity. We need one another. Our kids need us both. When we enjoy parenting as a team, we are most ful-filled, and our kids are the winners. "A cord of three strands is not easily broken," says the Master Designer. And a home with a healthy mom and a healthy dad wrapped around the Living Lord is a home not easily broken. It's a home where the sons grow like "strong trees" and the daughters become like "pillars adorning a palace."

British psychiatrist John Bowlby tells of a study by Main and Weston focusing on the importance of a child's bonding with both parents: "Children with a secure relationship to both par-ents were most confident and most competent; children who had a secure relationship to neither were least so; and those with a secure relationship to one parent but not to the other came in between."[2]

What are some of the differences between men and women that combine to make for the most effective parenting? My husband, Stu, pointed out some of them in his book *Tender Warrior:* "A woman is more delicate. She's the fine china, not the stoneware. She's a finely-tuned sports car, not a '66 Chevy pickup with mud flaps. She's more fragile, more sensitive. She has a more precisely adjusted sensory ability, especially in terms of relationships. A woman is more alert to what's happening in her environment."[3]

This detailed-oriented beauty is tender and gentle. A woman's verbal communication skills generally rise above her man's. Cyclical changes continually bring reminders of difference. The nurturing instinct causes her to believe, trust, and give.

Does God have an obvious sense of humor by literally developing opposite sides of the brain between teammates? We operate on different frequencies. We need a good translation. Our men have a task orientation that equips them to make necessary decisions. They are so logical, two plus two equals four, with no variations. "Men are like soldiers. They have to do painful and dangerous things without question. As a result, they become numb to their feelings."[4]

Because of all this, a man is equipped to be our initiator, leader, provider, and protector. He takes risks for the family and operates with a big picture. How essential it is for us to get a grip on the definition of masculinity!

How good that we're different! And how effective we can be when we identify those differences to understand our teamwork better! The sooner we learn this, the more prepared we are to live comfortably together and enjoy being the complement to our incredibly different teammates that God intended us to be.

In light of the importance of that teamwork, I give you

another avenue by which you can be a truly incredible mom—
love your husband. Really love him. Study your man. Learn
how he works. Adjust to him. Any good teammate would.
Accept him, join hands, and "go for it" together. (Love dissolves
a multitude of inadequacies.)

I have a friend who has caught this principle and practices it
consistently. Consequently, her home is a great place to be—
especially for the children. Listen to Rachel's wisdom, and follow it. *Make your husband your priority.*

> Many times, we women don't nurture our first rela-
> tionship in the home, our husbands. Children come
> along, and they become the focal point of the
> home. Their demands are the first ones met. Their
> pleasures are the first ones addressed. Meanwhile,
> there sits Dad.
>
> In all the long hours at the store and the adja-
> cent small business we ran as I grew up, I never
> wondered what was priority in my mother's life.
> God was first, her husband was second, and her
> kids were next.
>
> I give my mom a lot of credit in this area. She
> loved and cared for my dad in such a way that we
> knew he was the most important person in her life
> on this earth. That gave me great stability. That
> gave our home a great amount of peace. Even in
> the little things like having supper on the table at a
> certain time—that was important to Dad, therefore
> it became important to Mom. She studied her man,
> and in turn, he treated her like a queen.
>
> Too few women study their men today. They do
> everything else instead. I've seen some friends who
> feel such a need to compete with their mates, and
> nobody gets anything out of that kind of situation.
> They tell their friends how insensitive he is, how

How good that we're different! And how effective we can be when we identify those differences to understand our teamwork better!

inept he is with the children, but they never stop to figure out why. They don't take the initiative in creating a climate where it's safe for him to be him. He's the brunt of their discussions, and he's fair game when he comes home to be attacked for all the inequities he's bestowed upon her.

The real issue is this: Are we studying the heartbeat of both our husband and children and then living a life based upon that knowledge for the good of all? That's how life at home becomes fulfilling.

The next foundational principle is equally profound—let him lead. "Ever seen an orchestra without a conductor? A boat with no rudder? A compass without a needle? Pretty pathetic. Nothing works right."[5]

Dad was designed for the primary leadership role in the family. Help him win at it. Help him lead by setting him up to do so. Show respect for his ways. Gently provide him with bits of information, little nuances of family relationships that are more likely understood from where your gifts lie than from his. Demonstrate confidence in his leadership. Back away from taking the reins at every juncture where you differ.

Our nation is filled with dysfunctional homes powerfully influenced by women who seldom acknowledge the positive role of the father in the children's lives. Those same homes often witness a dad who shrivels, drops into a passive mode, and lets his leadership role go. And the dysfunction will show up in the next generation.

Richard Strauss tells us,

> When dad abdicates his position of authority in the home, mom usually assumes the role she was never intended to have. The unhappy combination of a disinterested father and an overbearing mother can drive children to run away from home, enter early

and unwise marriages, or suffer emotional difficulties and personality deficiencies. Dad must take the lead. . . .

A dominant wife and mother confuses the children. . . . If mothers and fathers have equal authority, the child does not know which one to obey. He will use one against the other to get his own way, and will soon lose respect for one or both parents. Studies have shown that children with conduct problems often have domineering, high-strung mothers. But if a child knows beyond all doubt that dad is the head of the house, that mom speaks for dad, and that dad's authority backs up what she says, he will be more apt to obey and will have more love and respect for both his parents.[6]

Help your husband succeed as a father. And listen again to what Rachel has to say about wives and mothers:

> We're described as helpmates in Scripture. I believe this is particularly true of our children's relationship with their father. Phil wasn't born with all the intuitions and insights into what kids are really saying, what they really mean, what they really want. It isn't that he doesn't want to know, he just doesn't come equipped with that "sixth sense."
>
> That's where we moms come into play. I feel we need to be gently helping our mates understand their children. Some guys have made an attempt, only to be ridiculed and criticized. Would you attempt that again if you were them? Probably not.
>
> My experience has been that when Phil is given the information to work with, he responds beautifully. "Dad, Marla's had a pretty hard day today. Her friends teased her about . . ." When Phil hears

this, in his own unique way, he meets her needs in a manner I could never dream of.

"Dad, Jason is really disappointed about the basketball team. He's thinking he'd like to drop out. What do you think?" Then I step away and let him have that moment with Jason.

A lot of women don't seem to acknowledge the positive role of the father in their children's lives. They only want to use him as a baby-sitter when they need to get away. We women have to make it a pleasure for them to get to know their children. Rather than feel like the male in our home is some-times our enemy, we need to truly see ourselves as team members together. We need to stop resenting our children's desire to be with their dads.

Many times I've been preempted because Dad was doing something else. That's okay. Contrary to what some mothers think, I can't be all things to my children. They need to have that relationship with their father in order to be balanced children. Phil wants to know his kids—they're his. Sometimes he just needs a little insight. If I see him as a threat, I've defeated myself in this great battle.

I feel strongly about Phil's place in our children's lives. They wouldn't be the same children today had it not been for their early exposure and contin-uing exposure to Phil and his abilities and wisdom as a father and man. He has brought a dimension to their lives that I'm thrilled about.

Phil and I aren't competing for their attention or affection. We're a team. I want my little girl to be a "daddy's girl." Nothing thrills me more than to see her at ease with her father, to see her tease and play with him, to see her seek comfort in his arms when the world seems brutal. The same is true with my sons. I loved it when I heard them discussing their muscles compared to their dad's. I loved it the day Jeff asked me, holding out his arms, if he was going to be as hairy "as my dad." My heart is warmed when Jason discusses how he watched his dad deal with a situation with patience and calmness.

Competition means dividing one's strength against another. It means overcoming your opponent. And it means there's a winner and a loser. That should have no place in a marriage. But when parenting is teamwork, and when you can help your partner succeed at parenting, everyone wins, especially your children.

Consider the words of Harvard psychiatrist Armand M. Nicholi II:

> Let me make an observation about the emotional health of a family. If any one factor influences the character development and emotional stability of an individual, it is the quality of the relationship he or she experiences as a child with both parents. . . . What has been shown to contribute most to the emotional development of the child is a close, warm, sustained, and continuous relationship with BOTH parents.[7]

So be a team player and love your husband—really love him. Make him your priority. Accept him. Let him lead. And help him succeed as a father. You'll win. He'll win. And most of all, your children will win.

Finally, a word to the single mom.
Unfortunately, you're not part of a marriage team. And as

much as you'd like to be, and despite your determination, you cannot be all things to your kids. Whether you have girls or boys, kids need a male role model in their lives. Look for influencers that can fill that void. As my little brother, Bruce, was growing up in our fatherless home, God brought three men— all named Don—into his life as father figures.

The first was the husband of the woman who baby-sat Bruce while Mom was at work. This man had meager means, but he taught Bruce how to work, how to fix things, and how to have fun in life even without money. The character he modeled and the unselfishness he showed were incredible.

The second Don was an uncle who took special interest in Bruce. Having lost his only child to death, this Don took it upon himself to be Bruce's encourager. He honored him on all the special days. He listened. He even gave up smoking when Bruce expressed his fear of losing him to cancer.

The third Don was a camp director where Mom worked. He saw to it that there were plenty of people in Bruce's life to encourage him, to nourish his soul, and to direct his activities.

Three very special influencers who helped fill the gap. If you're a single mom, look for the same kind of loving, selfless men to meet your children's need.

Mom, your potential for blessing your children is incredible. When joined with your husband's potential, it's even more incredible. None of us can do it alone. And even together, we'll always be working with both strengths and weaknesses. But as we say at our house, "We will never do things perfectly around here, but we will always do them together." I hope that becomes your commitment, too.

Afterword

How Does God Fit In?

ow does God fit into our mothering? "He doesn't," someone may respond impatiently. "If you're going to start that God talk, I'm not reading any further."

I understand. Motherhood isn't the only thing that hasn't gotten much good press lately. To some, the words *Christian* and *hypocrite* have become almost synonymous. And Christianity is being portrayed by the media and Hollywood more and more as an enclave for small-minded, bigoted people. But there's another side to the story. So even if you feel God has no place in your life, will you bear with me for just a moment or two?

Do you despise your wedding ring because someone manufactures imitations made of brass or plastic? Have you thrown out your leather handbag because so many stores now sell "genuine imitation cowhide"? Do you refuse to drink fresh-squeezed orange juice because companies have perfected imitation fruit flavors?

It's no wonder the Christian community has so many charlatans. And it should be of little surprise to learn that there are hypocrites in every church in every town in America.

It has always been true that only the precious things are imitated—gold, pearls, gemstones, great paintings, and other things of high value. Who do you know in the imitation paper business or the imitation garbage business? People always imitate those things that are most precious. But you don't throw out your prized possessions because there are imitations around. Nor should we throw out the opportunity for a personal relationship with God because there are fakers in our midst.

The hypocrites coming out of churches should be no surprise. They've simply become aware of their obvious needs, and they're going somewhere to have them dealt with. If we used the same approach to hospitals that we use with churches, many people would never go near a doctor or a hospital again. "You say you make people well. Hah! I've been watching who passes through your doors, and they're *all* sick."

The truth is, despite all the charlatans, all the hypocrites, and all the glitzy fakers who beg for your money on TV or loudly condemn you on a street corner, there is a place for God in your life—a precious place. It's a place where you can find open arms even if you're "sick" with the stains of the world and sick of yourself.

Knowing there are plastic rings makes your wedding band no less valid or valuable. Knowing there are pseudo-Christians clamoring for attention makes my faith no less precious to me. It's a treasure I would like to share with you.

How does God fit in? He fits very well right at the core of my being.[1] There is little space in this book on motherhood to tell you all you might want to know about having a relationship with God. But that's the answer you need above all else.[2]

Our holy God long ago condemned evil and all it spawns. Then He turned to us in compassion and said, "You can't overcome it, can you? It's part of you from infancy.[3] But I love you, so I'm going to provide an Overcomer for you—My Son.[4] He will resist evil. There won't be found in Him any sin at all.[5] And after He has proved it, I'll sacrifice His life in your place. He'll pay the price for your soul with His life's blood."[6]

Of course, that Overcomer's name is Jesus. And after Jesus was executed by being nailed to a wooden cross and then was buried hastily in a borrowed grave, God the Father brought Him back to life. He overcame evil and sin and even death.[7] The price He paid, He paid for you. He had no sin in His life to pay for. Everything He endured was for you. And all you have to do to receive this amazing gift is just to believe it.[8]

"For God so loved the world that he gave his one and only Son, that whoever believes in him shall not perish but have eternal life."[9]

"Whoever believes in the Son has eternal life, but whoever rejects the Son will not see life, for God's wrath remains on him."[10]

That's the choice set before you. And your answer to the question of whether you believe or not will dictate not only the life you live now, but your eternal destiny as well.

When God created us, He knew what we needed for the enjoyment of an abundant life.[11] He issued us a plan to follow in the Bible. To the extent we follow His guidelines, we'll be able to enjoy His intended peace and fulfillment.[12] To the extent we choose to go our own way, we'll be left to experience the consequences of our own selfish decisions.[13] The choice is ours.[14] How does God fit into your life?

When we speak of being a good parent, of being a nurturer and encourager, there's no better model than God Himself. Who loves like God? Who has sacrificed more than God? Who has provided for our future more than God?

He has given us life. He is the sustainer of life—He provides every breath we take.[15] He's the one who longs for our friendship with Him. He's the one who will always sit with us through our pain, our sorrow, our fear. He's our comforter. He's the one who nudges us toward good things and warns us, through our conscience, away from evil things.

He's the one who is always forgiving, always loving, always waiting.[16] He enjoys our growth and aches with us over our pains. He is *for* us.[17]

He's the ideal Father, and He wants to enjoy a relationship with you. When you believe Him and let Him live through you, you'll find peace and fulfillment such as you never imagined.

Think for a moment about the perfect mother. What characteristics would describe her? Maybe humble, wise, content, generous, self-sacrificing, peaceful, gentle, loving. But wait a minute. How can that be? How can she be content and peaceful if she has been sacrificing, giving, and loving? What about her fulfillment? What about her rights?[18]

It only makes sense that if we're going to be happy, we have to make sure we're getting our needs and desires fulfilled, right? And if we're humble, self-sacrificing, and generous, someone's going to take advantage of us, right? No, not really.[19]

That's why we need God. The world around us tells us we have to look out for number one, demand our rights, and stand up for ourselves.[20] Then we'll be happy. The result has been people who are more and more self-centered and selfish and yet, at the same time, less satisfied and still unhappy.

God tells us to go just the opposite direction of what seems so logical. He says to think more of others than ourselves, to give ourselves away, and to be generous, forgiving, and loving.[21] He says that in being concerned for others, we'll find ourselves satisfied,[22] whereas in being concerned only for ourselves, we'll never be satisfied.

Doesn't your image of the perfect mother prove it? It's her generous, sacrificing spirit you love so much. It's her humility you respect so highly. It's her generous, forgiving spirit that draws you to her.[23]

That's not logical to a world demanding its rights.[24] But it makes all the sense in the world (literally) to someone who stops and really thinks it through from God's perspective.[25] You see, real living is not a matter of how we experience this moment. If it were, we should all seek immediate self-gratification, live for the moment, and satisfy our appetites. Instead, it's a journey to be enjoyed all along the way, not just at this

The selfish road leads us to walk alone, pursuing all we can gather into our arms. The godly road leads us to walk with and care for others and to walk with God. In doing so, we find all the peace and fulfillment that others grab for in vain.

moment or just for the goal. The selfish road leads us to walk alone, pursuing all we can gather into our arms. The godly road leads us to walk with and care for others and to walk with God. In doing so, we find all the peace and fulfillment that others grab for in vain.[26]

Too many people live by the me-first philosophy. And though they see no relationship between it and the strengthening or weakening of their character, it has its destructive effects.[27]

A couple of years ago, we learned we had carpenter ants under our house. The house looked fine. So why bother about a few ants in the crawl space? Because they were eating away at the foundation of our home. Left unattended, they would have destroyed the beams and sills. Imagine ants actually being a physical danger to us! So it is with the me-first philosophy.

A friend I'll call Susie had always wanted children. Her husband, Pete, kept putting her off, saying they needed to wait until they were financially secure. After 17 years of marriage, Pete still wasn't ready for kids. In fact, he lost interest in Susie and their marriage entirely and had an affair.

Interestingly, the single woman he eventually left Susie for had two children of her own. Soon another was on the way—Pete's baby.

Now caught up in the excitement of a passionate relationship with Pete, the other woman began to feel hindered with the care of her two sons. She actually ended up giving away her sons for Pete. The grandparents took over by default because the children were otherwise abandoned.

Pete was out to satisfy himself first. After all, he deserved to find fulfillment. He never found it, I'm sure. But his pursuit was a costly one. It cost my friend Susie 17 years of marriage, betrayal, infidelity, no children, no family, and perhaps no chance now to have children. It cost the other woman her children, her self-respect, and her future with her family. And it certainly hurt the two sons who were discarded along the way.

The foundation was eaten away, and when things came crashing down, the destruction was great.[28]

Selfishness never results in self-fulfillment, only frustration.[29]

When I was in my late thirties, I became very frustrated. The great dread disease puberty had descended upon our home, and energy levels and emotions ran high. I seemed to be on overload just trying to deal with it all. I was pretty much known either as Stu's wife or as Kent, Blake, or Ryan's mom. I didn't have a job. I wasn't making an impact "out there" somewhere. I was "just" someone's wife or mother.

The thought ran through my mind, *What's all this getting me?* My thinking had grown clouded, and that cloud loomed over my emotions and sense of self-worth. The me-first philosophy was trying to eat away at my character.

I knew I had to stop and redirect my thinking. It was becoming too easy to fall into self-pity and discount my worth and the importance of what I was doing. So what was the answer? I needed some balance in my life. After all, those feelings had come for some reason. Though I didn't want to focus too much on myself, neither could I just stuff my feelings, play the martyr, and struggle on.

I learned that God says it's okay to take care of self,[30] just don't become self-obsessed. So I began to care for myself, planning diversions, breaks, and refreshing moments. I began to care more about my health, to make sure I got enough rest, exercise, and nourishment. I started taking more care in our marriage, too.[31] That can easily be taken for granted in the flurry of raising a family. And most of all, I began to listen more carefully to my Lord than to my world about who I was and what I was doing as a mother.[32]

God reminds me of my worth to Him when I don't feel

much appreciated.[33] He reminds me of the value of what I do when others look down on my role as "just" a mother.[34] He helps me see the goal out there in the future so I guard my steps more carefully today and tomorrow.[35]

His Word tells me He understands my sacrifices.[36] His presence assures me I'm not alone.[37] His example teaches me there are lasting rewards for my faithfulness that will far outshine running after selfish appetites.[38]

He is my example.[39] He's my friend.[40] He's my nurturer.[41] He's my biggest fan.[42] He's my hope.[43] He's my anchor in a storm.[44] He's my guide when I don't know where I'm headed.[45] He's my comforter.[46] He's my source of peace, contentment, and joy. He's everything.[47]

How does God fit in? He's essential.[48] Whether you've never stopped to even think much about God or you've been a Christian most of your life, let me encourage you—seek God. Don't just concede His existence or pay Him lip service. Don't just fill your life with busyness for God. But seek *Him*. Really stop and seek after a personal relationship with Him, and let Him begin to comfort and direct you.

Finally, I would encourage you to seek a mentor. Find a Christian woman you can really talk to. Someone you can trust. Someone who wants to help you grow.

In *Mothering Upstream*, Virelle Kidder says: "A mother without a mentor is walking a lonely road. She needs an older woman who will be her encouragement, her coach, her confidant. If you don't have a mentor, pray to find one. If you are older and hear God speaking to you about being someone's mentor, please take time to listen."[49]

I well remember what a mentor meant to me when Stu was

in the military and we were stationed in Germany. I was expecting our first child, I was thousands of miles from home, and I had no family or close friends nearby. Providentially, another officer's wife in our building took an interest in me and helped this new mom-to-be know what to expect along the way.

Stu was many miles away when I experienced the tragedy of a miscarriage. But that dear woman was by my side to instruct, encourage, and comfort me through the trauma. When I got pregnant again, she was forever there, cheering me up and sharing her hard-earned wisdom as a mother. I don't think I would have made it through that period without her.

Because mothering is like sowing seeds, you often don't see the fruits right away. It takes time to reap the reward. There are no guarantees, either. But if you do your best, relying on God for wisdom and strength, there's a good chance that your day to see wonderful fruit will come.

After 24-plus years of giving myself to the enrichment of my children's lives, it's encouraging to see and read the difference my efforts have made. When a secure young woman asks my son, "What makes you so confident?" I smile. His confidence seems too good to be true. But I remember the many experiences through which that self-assurance was developed.

My file of "keeper letters" continues to grow now that our boys are old enough to appreciate what Stu and I did for them. I'll quote just a couple of them here, not to boast but to encourage you with the thought that if your children are still young, your day to get such letters will come, too, if you'll hang in there.

One son wrote, "Mom, you're the greatest. I'd like to thank you for being the ultimate mom. There are none better. You've always been the caring person there to love us. Thanks also for being a forgiving person. Living with boys is different. Boys can be pretty harsh sometimes and say things they really don't mean. But you've always forgiven us. Thanks for everything. I seriously love you."

Another keeper said, "Mom, I love you, and if no one else ever recognizes you and thanks you for the work you've put into me—Mom, I thank you. I thank you for the lifelong investment you made by training and shaping me!"

Such fruits of mothering will override the difficult earlier times. But Mom, you've got to look beyond the immediate challenges and keep those future fruits in view. May I encourage you to look as much as 500 years into the future, because you can not only have a tremendous positive influence on your children now, but you can also bless multiple generations yet to be born. How's that for a big job worthy of the best efforts you can give?

How does God fit into my mothering? Very, very well. And I hope He fits very well into your life and mothering as well. He has brought me and my family to this point, and He will carry my children into the years ahead. Let Him do the same for you and those you love.

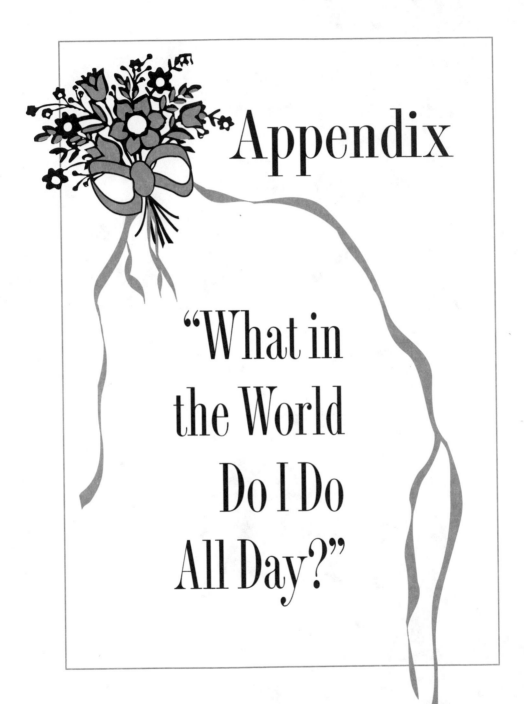

Appendix

"What in the World Do I Do All Day?"

*y husband comes home and wants to know what* I've done today. He'd better be careful how he asks such a question. He's had a demanding day, too, but somehow it's hard for him to relate to what it's been like at home. After all, this isn't "a real job."

Wait a minute! We moms all know better. Being a mom is a job with a capital J. We work our fingers to the bone, push our nerves to the edge, and use every skill possible to accomplish the demands of the day.

Just what does a mother do all day? Today's college student can't imagine. Numbers of women are baffled by what they'd do with "all that time" if they *had* to be home. Sometimes Mom herself can't remember.

In chapter 3, we saw the list sent to Ann Landers detailing some of the things moms are called on to do—things that make a difference. But there's so much more.

It's the little things that matter to our kids, the things that meet special needs, that say I love you. But if our lives become too fragmented by competing demands, little things like those can begin to slip through the cracks and be lost. Do they really make a difference? You bet they do.

Maybe you should make a list of your own. You might be surprised at all the differences you can make. What am I? Well, I'm the following:

- baby feeder, changer, bather, rocker, burper, hugger
- listener to crying and fussing and thousands of questions
- picker-upper of food and debris cast on the floor

- problem solver, determiner of action, and the one who gives those talks to whoever needs them
- phone messenger, the reminder of responsibilities
- comforter, encourager, counselor
- hygienist
- linguistic expert for two-year-old dialects
- trainer of baby-sitters
- listener—for the husband as well as the children— about their day, their needs, their concerns, their aspirations
- teacher of everything from how to chew food to how to drive a car
- assistant on school projects (collecting bugs, building papier-mâché volcanoes, etc.)
- questioner, prober to promote thinking
- censor of TV, movies, and books
- homework helper
- reader of thousands of children's books (over and over and over)
- planner and hostess of children's birthday parties
- planner and hostess of adult dinner parties (for friends, relatives, travelers, strangers, and for groups up to 100 at our home)
- short-order cook for those meals after the family's dinner that budding athletes depend upon
- room and board provider for someone in need, some- times for a night, sometimes forever, it seems
- central control for getting the appliance fixed or the carpet shampooed
- executioner of ants, roaches, wasps, and other pests
- resident historian in charge of photo albums, baby books, and school record books (at my house, I'm on book 58)
- resident encyclopedia source for all those hard questions that seem to arise

- officer of the day, on call for any emergency at home or away
- defroster of the freezer
- food preservation expert
- family secretary, confirming dinner reservations, travel, accommodations
- corresponder to the sick, the celebrating, or the generous
- archivist for everything that "must" be kept
- keeper and locater of birth certificates and other valuable documents
- ironer of wrinkles
- keeper and copier of tax forms (the preparer besides)
- appointment desk for the family's visits to the doctor, the dentist, the orthodontist, the barber, and the mechanic
- seeker of God, one who prays
- fitness expert
- front desk to keep track of each family member's daily itinerary
- cleaner of the oven, the drawers, the closets, the garage, the curtains, the bedding, the windows, even the walls
- waxer of cars
- refinisher of furniture
- hubby's romantic, attentive spouse
- enjoyer of those moments when nothing is happening, no one is calling, nothing demands attention— those rare, rare moments
- emergency medical technician and "ambulance" driver

And what else do I do? Well, among many other things, I do the following:

- clip ten fingernails and ten toenails for each young child regularly

- return library books
- get film developed
- choose gifts, purchase gifts, wrap gifts for birthdays, Christmas, Father's Day, Mother's Day, wedding showers, baby showers, anniversaries, and any other event that might even remotely require a gift (for me, that's at least 175 gifts a year to find)
- mail packages, buy stamps
- drop off the dry cleaning; pick up the dry cleaning
- get tennis rackets restrung
- have pictures framed
- haul everything that needs repair
- attend recitals
- attend every school sporting event imaginable
- chauffeur everyone everywhere
- cover for my sick kid on his 4:00 A.M. paper route
- comb little girl hairdos
- replace every battery in everything that ticks, whirls, or beeps
- help in the classroom
- become a mandatory volunteer for every fundraising drive
- participate in most school committees or boards
- attend school PTA meetings and conferences
- act as a room mother, making things and organizing *more* parties
- chaperon field trips and special events
- coordinate carpools (it makes men shudder)
- serve as a Scout leader, a Blue Bird leader, an AWANA leader, a Sunday school teacher
- purchase most everything for the family and the home
- keep relationships healthy with friends and every member on both sides of the family
- deliver forgotten lunches, forgotten homework, forgotten athletic gear

- attend church, Bible studies, committee meetings, showers, weddings, choir practices, board meetings, potlucks, and neighborhood meetings just to "stay active and informed"
- return everything everyone buys and then decides he doesn't like, doesn't need, or doesn't want
- make bank deposits and withdrawals
- save lives—sometimes figuratively, maybe literally

In my favorite book, the Bible, in Proverbs 31, it says, "An excellent wife, who can find? For her worth is far above jewels." She looks out for her family in many visible and tangible ways, and she just keeps working.

What in the world does an incredible mom do all day? All of this—and much more.

NOTES

Chapter Two

1. Louis M. Notkin, ed., *Mother Tributes from the World's Great Literature* (New York: Samuel Curl, 1943), p. 117.
2. Mabel Bartlett and Sophia Baker, *Mothers—Makers of Men* (New York: Exposition Press, 1952), p. 92.

Chapter Three

1. Ann Landers, May 1988.
2. Paraphrased from Rick Taylor, *When Life Is Changed Forever by the Death of Someone Near* (Eugene, Ore.: Harvest House, 1992), pp. 14-17.

Chapter Four

1. Ray Guarendi, *Back to the Family: How to Encourage Traditional Values in Complicated Times* (New York: Villard Books, 1990), pp. 121-22.
2. Ibid.
3. As quoted by Ellie Kahan, "20 Ways to Make Your Kid Feel Great," *Parents*, June 1990, p. 95.
4. Ibid.
5. Ann Ortlund, *Children Are Wet Cement* (New York: Revell, 1978), p. 58.

Chapter Five

1. Ann Landers, *The Oregonian*, November 18, 1990.

Chapter Six

1. Robert Lewis and William Hendricks, *Rocking the Roles* (Colorado Springs, Colo.: NavPress, 1991), pp. 212-13.
2. John Markle, "Text of Markle Letter," *Arkansas Democrat*, April 18, 1989, p. 11A.
3. Lewis and Hendricks, *Rocking the Roles*, pp. 212-13.
4. Brenda Hunter, *Home By Choice* (Portland, Ore.: Multnomah, 1991), pp. 59-60.

Chapter Seven

1. Proverbs 11:14 (*New American Standard Bible*).
2. Patricia Daniels Cornwell, *A Time for Remembering: The Story of Ruth Bell Graham* (San Francisco: Harper & Row, 1983), p. 229.

Chapter Eight

1. Brenda Hunter, *Home By Choice* (Portland, Ore.: Multnomah, 1991), p. 52.
2. Ibid, p. 62.
3. J. Conrad Schwarz, Robert G. Strickland, and George Krolick, "Infant Day Care: Behavioral Effects at Preschool Age," *Developmental Psychology*, 10 (1974), pp. 502-6.
4. Ron Haskins, "Public School Aggression Among Children with Varying Day Care Experience," *Child Development*, 56 (1985), pp. 689-700.
5. Hunter, *Home By Choice*, p. 64.
6. Sigmund Freud, *Outline of Psychoanalysis*, SE 23 (London: Hogarth Press, 1940), p. 188. Quoted in Hunter, *Home By Choice*, p. 26.
7. John Bowlby, *Attachment*, vol. I of *Attachment and Loss*, 2nd ed. (New York: Basic Books, 1982), p. xiii.
8. Judith Viorst, *Necessary Losses* (New York: Simon & Schuster, 1986), p. 31.
9. Hunter, *Home By Choice*, p. 28.

10. Richard Strauss, *How to Raise Confident Children* (Grand Rapids, Mich.: Baker, 1986), p. 133.
11. John Bowlby, address given to the American Psychiatric Association in Washington, D.C., 1986. Quoted in Hunter, *Home By Choice*, p. 46.

Chapter Nine

1. Elisabeth Elliot, "A Cheerful Word for Mothers at Home," quoting Brenda Sawyer of Twinsburg, Ohio, *Elisabeth Elliot's Newsletter,* July/August 1991, p. 2.
2. Mary Ann Froehlich, *What's a Smart Woman Like You Doing in a Place Like This?* (Brentwood, Tenn.: Wolgemuth & Hyatt, 1989), p. 163.
3. Ibid., p. 24.

Chapter Ten

1. Ingrid Groller, "Women and Work," *Parents*, June 1990, p. 108.
2. Jill Brooke Coiner, "Hey Hey Paula: The Secret to Paula Zahn's Balancing Act," *Family Circle*, June 8, 1993, p. 26.
3. Ibid.
4. Connie Marshner, *Can Motherhood Survive?* (Brentwood, Tenn.: Wolgemuth & Hyatt, 1990), p. 2.
5. Harry Stein, "Wisdom of Our Elders," *New Choices for Retirement Living,* July-August 1992, p. 43.
6. James Dobson, as quoted at a FamilyLife Conference.

Chapter Eleven

1. James Dobson and Gary Bauer, *Children At Risk* (Dallas: Word, 1990), p. 157.
2. J.M. Greenstein, "Father Characteristics and Sex Typing," *Journal of Personality and Social Psychology,* 3 (1966), pp. 271-77.
3. E.M. Hetherington, "Developmental Study of the Effects of the Sex of the Dominant Parent on Sex-Role Preference

Identification and Imitation in Children," *Journal of Personality and Social Psychology,* 2 (1965), pp. 188-94.

Chapter Twelve

1. Evie, "A Little Song of Joy for My Little Friends," *Why Complain* (Waco, Tex.: Word, 1978).
2. As quoted in Charles Swindoll, *The Grace Awakening* (Dallas: Word, 1990), pp. 5-6.
3. Ann Landers, *The Oregonian,* May 1990.

Chapter Thirteen

1. J. David Branon, "Sharing the Load," *Our Daily Bread,* June 1993, no. 3.
2. John Bowlby, *A Secure Base* (New York: Basic Books, 1988), p. 10.
3. Stu Weber, *Tender Warrior* (Sisters, Ore.: Multnomah, 1993), pp. 121-22.
4. Joan Shapiro, *Men, a Translation for Women* (New York: Dutton, 1992), p. 220.
5. Weber, *Tender Warrior,* p. 45.
6. Richard Strauss, *How to Raise Confident Children* (Grand Rapids, Mich.: Baker, 1986), pp. 120, 131.
7. Armand M. Nicholi II, "The Fractured Family: Following It into the Future," *Christianity Today,* May 25, 1979, p. 12.

Afterword

1. Psalm 139:1-18.
2. James 2:5; Matthew 6:8; 2 Timothy 2:7.
3. Psalm 51:3-5; Romans 7:17-21.
4. John 3:16.
5. Matthew 3:13 – 4:11.
6. Romans 5:8-21.
7. 1 Corinthians 15:3-28.
8. John 1:12.
9. John 3:16.

10. John 3:36.
11. John 10:10*b*.
12. Joshua 1:7.
13. Galatians 6:7-8.
14. Joshua 24:15.
15. Acts 17:25.
16. 1 John 1:9.
17. Romans 8:31.
18. James 4:10.
19. 1 Corinthians 2:14; Philippians 2:2-11; 1 Corinthians 3:18-19.
20. 2 Timothy 3:1-5.
21. Matthew 5:39-48.
22. John 12:24-26; Luke 17:33; Acts 20:35; Philippians 2:3-8; 1 Peter 5:5-6.
23. Proverbs 31:28.
24. 2 Corinthians 4:4.
25. 2 Corinthians 4:6.
26. Philippians 4:7.
27. Philippians 2:2-5; Proverbs 16:18; Proverbs 28:26.
28. Philippians 3:19.
29. Philippians 3:18-19.
30. 1 Peter 3:3-4; 1 Corinthians 3:16.
31. Titus 2:4-5.
32. 1 Chronicles 28:9*b*.
33. Ephesians 2:10.
34. Proverbs 31:10, 28.
35. Hebrews 13:5*b*; Psalm 23.
36. Galatians 6:9.
37. Hebrews 13:5*b*.
38. Proverbs 11:18.
39. Psalm 26:3.
40. John 15:15.
41. Hebrews 13:21.
42. Psalm 27:1.
43. Psalm 39:7.

44. Hebrews 6:19.
45. Psalm 48:14.
46. 2 Corinthians 1:3-7.
47. Psalm 18:2.
48. Colossians 1:17.
49. Virelle Kidder, *Mothering Upstream* (Wheaton, Ill.: Victor, 1990), p. 32.

For information about Linda Weber's speaking schedule or about having her speak to your group, write her at the following address:

Linda Weber
2229 NE Burnside St., #212
Gresham, OR 97030